READINGS ON

FRANKENSTEIN

THE GREENHAVEN PRESS

Literary Companion

TO BRITISH LITERATURE

READINGS ON

FRANKENSTEIN

Don Nardo, *Book Editor*

David L. Bender, *Publisher*
Bruno Leone, *Executive Editor*
Bonnie Szumski, *Series Editor*

Greenhaven Press, Inc., San Diego, CA

Every effort has been made to trace the owners of copy-righted material. The articles in this volume may have been edited for content, length, and/or reading level. The titles have been changed to enhance the editorial purpose. Those interested in locating the original source will find the complete citation on the first page of each article.

Library of Congress Cataloging-in-Publication Data

Readings on Frankenstein / Don Nardo, book editor.
     p.   cm. — (The Greenhaven Press literary companion to British literature)
    Includes bibliographical references and index.
    ISBN 0-7377-0183-8 (lib. bdg. : alk. paper). — ISBN 0-7377-0182-X (pbk. : alk. paper)
    1. Shelley, Mary Wollstonecraft, 1797–1851. Frankenstein. 2. Science fiction, English—History and criticism. 3. Horror tales, English—History and criticism. 4. Frankenstein (Fictitious character) 5. Scientists in literature. 6. Monsters in literature. I. Nardo, Don, 1947– . II. Series.
PR5397.F73R43 2000
823'.7—dc21
                                        99-29029
                                           CIP

Cover photo: American Stock/Archive Photos

Copyright © 2000 by Greenhaven Press, Inc.
PO Box 289009
San Diego, CA 92198-9009
Printed in the U.S.A.

"*All men hate the wretched; how, then, must I be hated, who am miserable beyond all living things! Yet you, my creator, detest and spurn me, thy creature, to whom thou art bound by ties only dissoluble by the annihilation of one of us. You purpose to kill me. How dare you sport thus with life?*"

The Monster to Victor Frankenstein in Chapter 10 of Mary Shelley's **Frankenstein**

CONTENTS

ence and how this potential can, for various reasons, become distorted, with the result that an inventor's creation can turn on him or her and blight humanity.

Chapter 2: Social and Psychological Themes in *Frankenstein*

Chapter 3: Stage and Film Adaptations of *Frankenstein*

novel *Frankenstein,* many of which have taken liberties with the original. In one version, for instance, the Monster dies in an avalanche; in another, he meets a fiery end in a volcano; in still another, he does not die at all. Indeed, some of these adapations are comedies!

Foreword

*"'Tis the good reader that
makes the good book."*

Ralph Waldo Emerson

The story's bare facts are simple: The captain, an old and scarred seafarer, walks with a peg leg made of whale ivory. He relentlessly drives his crew to hunt the world's oceans for the great white whale that crippled him. After a long search, the ship encounters the whale and a fierce battle ensues. Finally the captain drives his harpoon into the whale, but the harpoon line catches the captain about the neck and drags him to his death.

A simple story, a straightforward plot—yet, since the 1851 publication of Herman Melville's *Moby-Dick*, readers and critics have found many meanings in the struggle between Captain Ahab and the whale. To some, the novel is a cautionary tale that depicts how Ahab's obsession with revenge leads to his insanity and death. Others believe that the whale represents the unknowable secrets of the universe and that Ahab is a tragic hero who dares to challenge fate by attempting to discover this knowledge. Perhaps Melville intended Ahab as a criticism of Americans' tendency to become involved in well-intentioned but irrational causes. Or did Melville model Ahab after himself, letting his fictional character express his anger at what he perceived as a cruel and distant god?

Although literary critics disagree over the meaning of *Moby-Dick*, readers do not need to choose one particular interpretation in order to gain an understanding of Melville's novel. Instead, by examining various analyses, they can gain numerous insights into the issues that lie under the surface of the basic plot. Studying the writings of literary critics can also aid readers in making their own assessments of *Moby-Dick* and other literary works and in developing analytical thinking skills.

The Greenhaven Literary Companion Series was created with these goals in mind. Designed for young adults, this unique anthology series provides an engaging and comprehensive introduction to literary analysis and criticism. The essays included in the Literary Companion Series are chosen for their accessibility to a young adult audience and are expertly edited in consideration of both the reading and comprehension levels of this audience. In addition, each essay is introduced by a concise summation that presents the contributing writer's main themes and insights. Every anthology in the Literary Companion Series contains a varied selection of critical essays that cover a wide time span and express diverse views. Wherever possible, primary sources are represented through excerpts from authors' notebooks, letters, and journals and through contemporary criticism.

Each title in the Literary Companion Series pays careful consideration to the historical context of the particular author or literary work. In-depth biographies and detailed chronologies reveal important aspects of authors' lives and emphasize the historical events and social milieu that influenced their writings. To facilitate further research, every anthology includes primary and secondary source bibliographies of articles and/or books selected for their suitability for young adults. These engaging features make the Greenhaven Literary Companion series ideal for introducing students to literary analysis in the classroom or as a library resource for young adults researching the world's great authors and literature.

Exceptional in its focus on young adults, the Greenhaven Literary Companion Series strives to present literary criticism in a compelling and accessible format. Every title in the series is intended to spark readers' interest in leading American and world authors, to help them broaden their understanding of literature, and to encourage them to formulate their own analyses of the literary works that they read. It is the editors' hope that young adult readers will find these anthologies to be true companions in their study of literature.

INTRODUCTION

A scientist scurries through his laboratory, which is atmospherically lit and cluttered with fantastic electronic machinery and other gadgets. Excited, almost crazed, and seemingly on the verge of some momentous discovery, he barks orders to his grizzled, hunchbacked assistant. The two focus their attention on a body lying on a table. It is a hideous conglomeration of parts from different human corpses. Soon, harnessing the mysterious powers of his machines and bolts of lightning from an angry-looking sky, the scientist animates the creature. It stirs, opens its eyes, and beholds its strange surroundings with a mixture of fear and confusion. In time it will turn on its creator, who will learn the lesson of meddling in God's affairs.

Scenes like this one, played out seemingly endlessly on movie and television screens for almost a century, are familiar to everyone, regardless of age, background, or economic or educational level. The scientist, as even a child in grade school will readily attest, is Dr. Frankenstein, who created life in a laboratory, who made the dead walk. His creation has come to be called Frankenstein too. This is an interesting and fitting twist; for in Mary Shelley's original novel, on which the Frankenstein films are based, the creation was portrayed as an extension—the son, or darker self—of the creator. Of course, the novel has no hunchbacked assistant and no angry villagers with torches chasing the Monster through the countryside; these and other now familiar images were added in subsequent adaptations. Yet nearly all later versions have retained the main characters and central concepts of Mary Shelley's original.

That these characters and central concepts have become not only world famous, but also cultural icons and facets of modern public consciousness is perhaps not surprising. First published in 1818, the novel (whose full title was *Frankenstein, or the Modern Prometheus*) was one of the best and most influential works of the English Romantic period of fiction writing. It dealt with such themes as individual and class alienation, the conflict between human intellect and emotion, the dark potential of misusing scientific advances, and the relationship between humans and God. And it did so in the then popular gothic (dark, mysterious, macabre) setting and style and presented characters and situations that were controversial, riveting, disturbing, and even terrifying for their time. "It produced shock and bewilderment," comments noted drama critic Christopher Small.

> When it first appeared its newness may fairly be called staggering. . . . There was something monstrous about its central idea that produced the typical reactions of people confronted with a *lusus naturae*, a breach in the accepted order of things.[1]

The novel and its "monstrous" central concept not only laid the groundwork for later speculative fiction involving scientific themes, but also immediately gave birth to an onslaught of stage and film adaptations that has not abated, nor even slowed, to this day. As University of Northumbria scholar Peter Hutchings suggests, "There is no such thing as *Frankenstein*, there are only *Frankensteins*, as the text is ceaselessly rewritten, reproduced, refilmed and redesigned."[2] It is therefore sometimes difficult to discern which ideas originated in the novel and which were later added to the growing "Frankenstein mythos" (the accumulation of characters, themes, symbols, and storylines based directly or loosely on the original, all circulating in the public or cultural consciousness). For these literary and cultural reasons, *Frankenstein* is widely taught in college and high school courses ranging from surveys of gothic fiction and science fiction to women's literature and the history of ideas.

The essays selected for the Greenhaven Literary Companion to Mary Shelley's *Frankenstein* provide teachers and students with a wide range of information and opinion about both the novel and its author. All of the authors of the essays are or were (until their deaths) English professors at leading colleges and universities, literary scholars and critics, theater and film historians, or noted biographers of Mary Shelley. Most of the essays deal specifically with the original novel, examining its conception and the sources, meanings, and implications of its themes and ideas. Because the novel's later stage and film adaptations have acquired a life of their own and are most often the medium through which the author's ideas are transmitted to society, the remainder of the essays explore the history of these adaptations and the degree to which they remain true to the original.

This companion to *Frankenstein* has several special features. Each of the essays explains or discusses in detail a specific, narrowly focused topic. The introduction to each essay previews the main points. And inserts interspersed within the essays serve as examples of ideas expressed by the authors, offer supplementary information, and/or add authenticity and color. These inserts come from *Frankenstein,* from critical commentary about the novel or its era, or from other scholarly sources. Above all, this companion is designed to enhance the reader's understanding and enjoyment of a story so ingrained in the popular mind that, as Small writes, it is on the one hand "uniquely new to every fresh generation of readers" and on the other "familiar to them before they begin to read."[3]

NOTES

1. Christopher Small, *Mary Shelley's* Frankenstein: *Tracing the Myth.* Pittsburgh: University of Pittsburgh Press, 1973, p. 13.
2. Peter Hutchings, *Hammer and Beyond: The British Horror Film.* New York: Manchester University Press, 1993, p. 98.
3. Small, *Mary Shelley's* Frankenstein, p. 13.

MARY SHELLEY AND
FRANKENSTEIN

According to its author, the main characters and central concept of *Frankenstein* were first conceived in a darkened room, with "closed shutters, with moonlight struggling through," and a "glassy lake and white high Alps beyond."[1] The majestic and highly romantic setting was an imposing villa, the Diodati, nestled along the shores of Lake Geneva, in Switzerland. The year was 1816, and Mary Godwin, a young Englishwoman of nineteen, and her soon-to-be husband, the English romantic poet Percy Bysshe Shelley, were paying a summer visit to another English poet, Lord (George Gordon) Byron, who had recently rented the villa.

It had been a "wet, ungenial [unfriendly] summer, and incessant rain often confined us for days to the house,"[2] Mary later recalled. To while away the time, Byron and his guests, who also included his handsome young doctor and friend, John Polidori, engaged in discussions of literature as well as various intellectual and often controversial topics. One night, not long after acquiring some German ghost stories that had been translated into French, Byron suddenly exclaimed, "We will each write a ghost story!" According to Mary's later recollection:

> There were four of us. The noble author [Byron] began a tale, a fragment of which he [later] printed at the end of his poem *Mazeppa* [published in 1819]. Shelley, more apt to embody ideas and sentiments in the radiance of brilliant imagery . . . commenced one founded on the experiences of his early life. Poor Polidori had some terrible idea about a skull-headed lady who was . . . punished for peeping through a keyhole. . . . I busied myself *to think of a story* . . . one which would speak to the mysterious fears of our nature and awaken thrilling horror—one to make the reader dread to look round, to curdle the blood and quicken the beatings of the heart. If I did not accomplish these things, my ghost story would be unworthy of its name.[3]

But for several days, Mary was unable to conceive of just the right story. More intellectual conversations ensued, one between Byron and Shelley about the nature and principle of life, the latest scientific discoveries, and whether such discoveries might allow a human to usurp God's role and create life. An eerie, almost spooky mood having been created, that night Mary retired to her room, the one with the "closed shutters with moonlight struggling through." Unable to sleep, all at once she was inundated by a flood of stark and disturbing ideas and images. "My imagination, unbidden, possessed and guided me," she wrote later,

> gifting the successive images that arose in my mind with a vividness far beyond the usual bounds of reverie [daydreaming]. I saw,—with shut eyes, but acute mental vision—I saw the pale student of unhallowed [unholy] arts kneeling beside the thing he had put together. I saw the hideous phantasm of a man stretched out, and then, on the working of some powerful engine [machine], show signs of life, and stir with an uneasy, half-vital motion.[4]

Frankenstein and his Monster had been born. As intelligent, educated, and inventive as she was, their creator could scarcely have imagined at that moment that these characters would become universally recognized cultural icons for generations yet unborn.

THE DAUGHTER OF CELEBRITIES

Indeed, the young woman whose principal ambition was to become a successful, well-known writer, would also have been surprised, and perhaps a bit disconcerted, to learn that her two most famous characters became much better known than she. That Mary Shelley would strive to become a writer seemed almost predestined. As she herself put it in her introduction to the 1831 edition of *Frankenstein*, "It is not singular [unusual] that, as the daughter of two persons of distinguished literary celebrity, I should very early in life have thought of writing."[5] The parents to whom she referred were William Godwin (1756–1836), an ex-minister turned atheist who became a renowned novelist and essayist; and Mary Wollstonecraft (1759–1797), a pioneering feminist writer. In works such as Godwin's *Enquiry Concerning Political Justice* (1793) and Wollstonecraft's *Vindication of the Rights of Woman* (1792), the couple, mavericks for their time, strongly advocated the concept of complete personal and intellectual freedom.

When William Godwin's and Mary Wollstonecraft's daughter Mary was born on August 30, 1797, in London, the mother already had a three-year-old daughter, Fanny, who had been born out of wedlock to an American merchant named Gilbert Imlay. Mary Wollstonecraft died of complications of childbirth only a few days after her second daughter's birth. This was the first of a series of tragic losses that Mary Godwin (later Mary Shelley) would endure in her relatively short lifetime. Her mother's untimely death left her father emotionally crushed with two young girls to raise on his own. Because he did not feel up to the task and also because he believed Mary and Fanny needed a mother, in 1801 he married his next-door neighbor, Mary Jane Clairmont. The new wife came to the marriage with two daughters of her own, including young Jane (later called Claire).

From the start, Mary Godwin did not get along with her new stepmother and stepsister Claire. And though the future author of *Frankenstein* dearly loved her father, for the rest of her life she could not help feeling that he had emotionally abandoned her in favor of his new family. A number of later scholars have suggested that Victor Frankenstein's rejection of the Monster, who is in a sense his son, is an expression and projection of the author's own deep-seated feelings. According to Mary's distinguished modern biographer, Anne K. Mellor, for example:

> The Monster's autobiographical account of a benevolent disposition [friendly nature] perverted by social neglect drew most directly on Mary Shelley's own experience of childhood abandonment and emotional deprivation in the Godwin household after her father's remarriage to the unsympathetic Mrs. Clairmont.[6]

CHILDHOOD INFLUENCES AND EDUCATION

Whatever her personal feelings, Mary Godwin did revere her father and was constantly reminded that she was the daughter of famous and gifted parents. A steady stream of intellectual giants visited the household during her childhood, some of whom she came to know well. These included poet Samuel Taylor Coleridge (author of "The Rime of the Ancient Mariner," which later became an important thematic source for *Frankenstein*); chemist Sir Humphry Davy (whose world-renowned experiments influenced the use of science in the novel); and writer Charles Lamb (author of the widely read *Tales from Shakespeare*). Hobnobbing with such figures was undoubtedly an education in itself. And in fact, Mary did not attend a formal school; instead, Godwin educated her at home. Her tutoring presumably followed the precepts Godwin outlined in an 1802 letter to a friend:

You enquire respecting the books I think best adapted for the education of female children from the age of two to twelve. I can answer you best on the early part of the subject, because in that I
have made the most experiments; and in that part I should make
no difference between children male and female. . . . I will put
down the names of a few books, calculated to excite the imagination, and at the same time quicken the apprehensions of children. The best I know is a little French book, entitled "Contes de
ma Mère, or Tales of Mother Goose." I should also recommend
"Beauty and the Beast," "Fortunatus," and a story of a queen and
country maid in . . . "Dialogues of the Dead." Your own memory
will easily suggest others . . . such as "Valentine and Orson" . . .
"Robinson Crusoe" . . . and the "Arabian Nights." I would undoubtedly introduce before twelve years of age some smattering
of geography, history, and the other sciences; but it is the train of
reading I have here mentioned which I should principally depend upon for generating an active mind and warm heart.[7]

Godwin so strongly encouraged his daughter's literary interests that in 1808, when she was only eleven, he published her
short book of verses titled *Mounseer Nongtongpaw; or the
Discoveries of John Bull in a Trip to Paris.*[8]

ENTER SHELLEY

Another intellectual visitor to the Godwin household was to
have a far more profound and lasting effect on Mary's life
than any other. He was poet Percy Shelley, who had been
greatly impressed and moved by Godwin's famous tract on
political justice. In 1814, at age nineteen, Shelley began making pilgrimages to Godwin's residence on London's Skinner
Street, where the two men engaged in fervent political and
literary talk. Mary, who had just returned from an almost
two-year stay with family friends in Scotland, was immediately smitten with the handsome, eloquent young poet; he
was equally drawn to her. They began taking long walks together and fell deeply in love. A shadow hung over the relationship, however, namely the fact that Shelley had a young
wife named Harriet and two young children by her, whom he
now all but abandoned for Mary.

William Godwin was livid at the discovery that his daughter was carrying on with a married man; Shelley's family was
similarly outraged. To escape the uncomfortable atmosphere, in July 1814 Mary and Shelley ran off to the Continent,
the common English term for the European mainland. With
them went Mary's stepsister Claire Clairmont, who supposedly wanted to share in what promised to be an exciting and
romantic adventure. But the trip turned out to be far from ex-

citing or romantic for all concerned. The three had little money and found traveling without it difficult and unrewarding. Moreover, Mary despised Claire's presence. "Now, I would not go to Paradise with her as a companion," Mary later wrote. "She poisoned my life when young . . . [and] she has still the faculty of making me more uncomfortable than any human being."[9]

The disenchanted travelers returned to England at the end of the summer. In February of the following year (1815), Mary had her first child, a daughter who died unnamed after a few days. (A few scholars maintain that the infant did receive a name—Clara.) It was a harrowing experience for the eighteen-year-old mother. In March, she had two morbid dreams about the dead child, recording in her journal:

> Dream[ed] that my little baby came to life again; that it had only been cold, and that we rubbed it before the fire, and it lived. Awake[d] and find no baby. I think about the little thing all day. Not in good spirits.[10]

Even if the incident had no influence on the later development of the central concept of *Frankenstein*, which is debatable, Mary's association of fire with bringing the dead to life was certainly a bizarre piece of coincidence and foreshadowing.

MARY CONCEIVES AND WRITES *FRANKENSTEIN*

Mary's gloom lifted somewhat when she soon became pregnant again. The apparently healthy child was born in January 1816, and she and Shelley named the boy William after Mary's father. In April, Mary's spirits received a further lift when Claire confided in her and Shelley an important secret. The renowned poet Lord Byron, whom Mary and Shelley greatly admired but had never met, had just left England for a rented villa in Switzerland. Shortly before his departure, he and Claire had become lovers; supposedly out of his strong feelings for Claire, Byron had invited Mary and Shelley to accompany Claire on an impending visit to Switzerland.

As it turned out, Claire's story was only partly true. She had indeed slept with Byron. But he was a notorious ladies' man, who had had intimate relations with dozens of women and, finding her mundane, had at first rebuffed her advances. To curry favor, she had promised to introduce him to the daughter of William Godwin, whom he held in high regard. In a convoluted scenario worthy of a soap opera, therefore, Byron had slept with Claire only for the chance to meet Mary.

This is how Mary, Shelley, their infant son William, and

Claire Clairmont ended up in Geneva in the summer of 1816. Mary and Shelley rented a villa only a ten-minute walk from Byron's larger and more elegant Villa Diodati, where the great epic poet John Milton had once stayed. After Mary had conceived the central characters and idea of her ghost story for the friendly competition with Shelley and the others, she "announced" to them "that I had *thought of a story.*" She later recalled how the work developed:

> At first I thought but a few pages—of a short tale; but Shelley urged me to develop the idea at greater length. I certainly did not owe the suggestion of one incident, nor scarcely of one train of feeling to my [later] husband, and yet but for his incitement it would never have taken the form in which it was presented to the world. From this declaration I must except the preface. As far as I can recollect, it was entirely written by him.[11]

Shelley did indeed write the preface to the novel, which Mary finished in May 1817. His preface is written in the first person, giving the natural impression that the person who wrote it wrote the novel as well. One passage reads, for instance:

> The circumstance on which my story rests was suggested in casual conversation. It was commenced partly as a source of amusement, and partly as an expedient for exercising any untried resources of mind. Other motives were mingled with these as the work proceeded. I am by no means indifferent to the manner in which whatever moral tendencies exist in the sentiments or characters it contains shall affect the reader; yet my chief concern in this respect has been limited to avoiding the . . . effects of the novels of the present day.[12]

With the intention of helping a young, inexperienced writer, Shelley also made several stylistic modifications. In various places in the text, for example, he changed "talked" to "conversed," "felt" to "endured," "hot" to "inflamed," "die" to "perish," and "ghost-story" to "a tale of superstition." Typical of some of his changes in longer phrases was his substitution of "a considerable time period elapsed" for her "it was a long time"; and his "in compliance with his favorite theory, that learning was superfluous in the commerce of ordinary life" for her "said he did not see of what use learning could be to a merchant."[13]

FRANKENSTEIN'S PUBLICATION AND CRITICAL RECEPTION

Shelley also helped Mary by making arrangements for the publisher Lackington, which had handled some of his own writings, to release the book. Perhaps because they felt that no publisher would take seriously a work produced by a teenaged girl, Mary and Percy decided it would be best to keep the author's identity a secret, so the novel was published anonymously in March 1818. Most people assumed that Shelley himself had written it.

Though the book proved a best-seller, the reviews were mixed. Some thought it sensational and trashy. The critic of the *Edinburgh Review* wrote:

> When we have thus admitted that *Frankenstein* has passages that appeal [to] the mind and make the flesh creep, we have given it all the praise (if praise it can be called) which we dare bestow. Our taste and judgment alike revolt at this kind of writing, and the greater the ability with which it may be executed, the worse it is.[14]

Somewhat kinder was the *Edinburgh Magazine*'s review, which stated, "There never was a wilder story imagined; yet, like most fictions of this age, it has an air of reality attached to it by being connected with the favorite [scientific] projects and passions of the times."[15] A few critics thought the book was exceptionally good; the *Blackwood's Edinburgh Magazine* reviewer (who, like most other people, thought Percy Shelley was the author), declared:

> Upon the whole, the work impresses us with the high idea of the author's original genius and happy power of expression. We shall be delighted to hear that he has aspired to *paullo majora* ["greater things," i.e., a work larger and more complex than his customary poems]; and in the meantime, congratulate our readers upon a novel which excites new reflections and untried sources of emotion.[16]

In a letter to a friend, Byron gave a private assessment, which, though perhaps biased by his friendship with the author, was insightful. "Methinks," he stated, "it is a wonderful work for a girl of nineteen,—*not* nineteen, indeed, at the time."[17]

FORESHADOWING FUTURE PROBLEMS AND CHALLENGES

Later generations of critics and readers, of course, have come heartily to concur with Byron. They have also praised the novel's originality, ingenuity of conception and execution, and discerning foreshadowing of some of the most significant scientific and social-psychological problems and challenges of modern technological civilization. Not the least of these is the tendency for some scientific discoveries and inventions to be used for *de*structive as well as *con*structive purposes, as in the case of nuclear energy. Victor Frankenstein's experiment, begun with good intentions but subsequently marred by terror and tragedy, thus symbolizes the potential perversion of scientific research. Summarizing the qualities that have given the novel its long life, Mary's noted modern biographer Elizabeth Nitchie writes:

> It is, to be sure, an amazing achievement for a girl of nineteen. But it is far more than that. It is no immature spinning of a "ghost story." The structure of the plot is remarkable in its symmetrical intricacy. The characters, showing sharp contrasts with each other and in themselves, are convincing in their combination of strangeness and reality. The descriptions of natural scenery have a power not greatly inferior to that of the poets who were Mary's contemporaries [i.e., Shelley and Byron]. The novel is interesting too . . . for its reflection of the contemporary thought in the fields of science and education, and most of all for its understanding of the tragedy of the creature who is "born with a different face," who can find no secure place in society.[18]

In their introduction to a 1963 edition of the novel, scholars R.E. Dowse and D.J. Palmer add this astute observation about its modernity and continuing relevance:

> *Frankenstein* is specifically modern in its dramatization of two important conceptions of humanity current in our time. On the one hand the liberal rationalist's [i.e., optimist's] belief in human kind's innate goodness, and in its ability to improve and control the conditions in which its natural tendency to good can flourish; and on the other hand the Romantic apprehension of a power beyond that of reason: the hidden power of the imagination which controls and determines humanity's moral nature, and which is the source of its creative energy. The story of Frankenstein and the Monster symbolizes the tension between these two views of the nature of the human being: Frankenstein is both the creator and the slave of his creature.[19]

Although the bulk of the novel's literary qualities and social relevance was not fully apparent to most people when it was first published, the story told in *Frankenstein* nonetheless touched a nerve in the public imagination. This was evidenced by the appearance in 1823 (only months after the release of the book's second edition and the disclosure that Mary, and not Percy, was the author) of the first of its thousands of stage (and later film) adaptations. The play, written by Richard B. Peake, was titled *Presumption; or the Fate of Frankenstein* and starred the then widely popular stage actors James Wallack and Thomas Potter Cooke as Frankenstein and the Monster, respectively.

SEVERAL UNFORTUNATE EVENTS

Meanwhile, writing and publishing two editions of *Frankenstein* was certainly not all that occupied Mary Godwin between 1816 and 1823. In late August 1816, Mary, Shelley, young William, and Claire Clairmont departed the Villa Diodati, where Mary had conceived the germinal elements of *Frankenstein*, and returned to England. Over the next several months, as Mary labored on what would prove to be her greatest literary work, she and Shelley were repeatedly distracted by crucial events, most of them unfortunate if not tragic. First, in October, Fanny Godwin, Mary's half-sister, committed suicide (and was buried anonymously because her father refused to identify or claim the body). Then, in December, Harriet Shelley's body turned up in a river. She too had taken her own life. Apparently the combination of the humiliation of her husband's abandonment, the strain of raising their two young children on her own, and the fact that she had recently become pregnant by another man was too much for her to bear.

Mary and Shelley now found themselves contemplating marriage. They had long viewed as unnecessary the traditional and formal legalization of their union. But Harriet's family was threatening to sue Shelley for custody of the children and his lawyers suggested that tying the knot with Mary might make him more respectable in the eyes of the courts. The ceremony took place on December 30, 1816, at St. Mildred's Church in London. Mary Godwin now officially became Mary Shelley. Her father, who had remained distant for some two years, was relieved and delighted. "According to the vulgar ideas of the world, she is well married" Godwin wrote to his brother,

> and I have great hopes the young man will make her a good husband. You will wonder, I dare say, how a girl without a penny of fortune should meet with so good a match. But such are the ups and downs of this world.[20]

But while the marriage pleased Godwin, it did not move the courts. In March 1817 Shelley lost custody of his and Harriet's children and the evidence suggests that he never saw them again.

A NEW SERIES OF TRAGEDIES

For Mary Shelley, the next few years provided ample confirmation of the "ups and downs of the world" of which her father had spoken. On the positive side, she traveled to the Continent, spending many pleasant months in Italy, and after *Frankenstein*'s publication early in 1818 she worked fairly steadily on two more novels, *Valperga* and *Mathilda*. On the negative side, these years were marred by intermittent tragedies. In September 1817, Mary gave birth to a daughter, whom she and Shelley named Clara Everina, but the child died of fever just over a year later. Then, in June 1819, when Mary was twenty-two, William, then three, died of malaria (or possibly cholera). Mary, who was already pregnant for a fourth time, suffered from deep depression for some time afterward. Her mood improved markedly after the new baby, Percy Florence, was born in November of that year. She did not yet know, of course, that he would be the only one of her children to survive into adulthood.

No tragedy Mary had endured so far in her life compared in significance, however, to that which struck in July 1822. Percy Shelley and a friend, Edward Williams, went sailing off the western Italian coast in Shelley's small boat, the *Don Juan*. An unexpected storm suddenly descended on the area, the boat disappeared, and for ten days teams of searchers combed the coastal beaches and inlets. On July 19, Mary was finally informed that the drowned bodies of the two men had been found washed up on a beach. Stoically, indeed undoubtedly in a state of shock, Mary visited the beach the next morning and viewed the three white sticks that marked her beloved's temporary grave. "I never saw such a scene—nor wish to see such another,"[21] was how Byron described Mary's mental and emotional state when he visited her a few weeks later.

Perhaps because she was so young and resilient, Mary somehow mustered the strength to survive the loss of her husband. One way of coping was, in a very real sense, to deify Shelley and his memory in the true and resplendent manner of the poets and other artists of the Romantic era. That process began almost immediately, as evidenced by this passage from a letter she wrote to a friend later in 1822:

> I was fortunate in having [been] fearlessly placed by destiny in the hands of one, who was a superior being among men, a bright planetary spirit enshrined in an earthly temple, raised me to the height of happiness—so far am I now happy that I would not change my situation as His widow with that of the most prosperous woman in the world—and surely the time will at length come when I shall be at peace & my brain & heart be no longer alive with unutterable anguish. I can conceive but of one circumstance that could afford me the semblance of content—that is the being permitted to live where I am now in the same house, in the same state, occupied alone with my child, in collecting His manuscripts—writing his life, and thus to go easily to my grave.[22]

Mary's efforts to glorify Percy Shelley's memory continued. She devoted herself over the following two years to the
collection, editing, and publication of his previously unpublished poems in a volume titled *Posthumous Poems of Percy
Bysshe Shelley.* But admirable as this and other such efforts
were, they served to isolate a young woman who, had she not
been so haunted by the dead, might have found a happy, ful-
filled life. "She overcompensated by recreating Percy Shelley
in the image of a living god," says Anne Mellor.

> And in so doing, she both denigrated [downplayed and belit-
> tled] herself and rendered it impossible to establish normal,
> healthy relationships with other men. Always the shadow of
> Percy Shelley came between them.[23]

This was surely the reason that Mary refused proposals of
marriage: in 1825 from John Howard Payne, an American
actor-manager, and in 1831 from Edward Trelawny, a friend
she and Percy had known in Italy.

HER ONLY MASTERPIECE

Percy Shelley continued to haunt Mary the rest of her days.
Some of her most important later writings contain tributes to
him, often in the guise of characters that are clearly modeled
on him. The novel *The Last Man,* published in 1826, for instance, features two characters, Adrian, earl of Windsor, and
Lord Raymond, who are much like Shelley and Byron (who
had died of fever, at age thirty-six, in Greece in April 1824).

Neither *The Last Man* nor any of Mary's other novels ever
matched the literary quality or public popularity of *Frankenstein.* Her inability to turn out another masterpiece in her
more mature years may have been partly the result of the
emotional roller-coaster that her long series of tragedies
forced her to ride. Some scholars suggest that it was the very
fact that when she conceived *Frankenstein* she was so young,
full of exuberance, and not yet encumbered by heavy worries
and responsibilities that gave the novel its power. In the view
of her biographer Muriel Spark:

> *Frankenstein* is Mary Shelley's best novel because at that age
> she was not yet well acquainted with her own mind. As her
> self-insight grew—and she was exceptionally introspective
> [absorbed in self-examination]—so did her work suffer from
> causes the very opposite of her intention; and what very often
> mars her later writing is its extreme explicitness [i.e., its de-
> tailed descriptions, leaving little to the imagination]. In
> *Frankenstein,* however, it is the implicit utterance [unstated
> ideas lurking beneath the narrative's surface] which gives the
> theme its power.[24]

Throughout the remainder of her life, Mary Shelley knew well that the tale of Victor Frankenstein and his monstrous creation was her most successful work. She may also have sensed that it was the best, for she labored diligently at refurbishing and rewriting it for the release of its third edition in 1831. It was for this edition that she penned the now famous and often quoted introduction explaining how a girl of nineteen had conceived such serious and hideous characters and ideas.

Mary lived long enough to see her son, Percy Florence, the only surviving relative or friend from her early life, grow up and marry (in 1848). After a series of strokes, she died in London on February 1, 1851, at the age of fifty-three. Her son saw that she was buried between the remains of her mother and father, whose creative talents she had inherited. Less than two years before, the fourth stage version of her most famous novel, a musical comedy titled *Frankenstein; or The Vampire's Victim*, had opened in London. No one at the time could have foreseen that the flood of flamboyant adaptations of the work that would ultimately make her immortal had only just begun.

NOTES

1. From the Introduction to the 1831 edition of *Frankenstein*, quoted in Marilyn Butler, ed., *Frankenstein or the Modern Prometheus*. New York: Oxford University Press, 1994, p. 196.
2. 1831 Introduction, in Butler, *Frankenstein*, p. 194.
3. 1831 Introduction, in Butler, *Frankenstein*, pp. 194–95.
4. 1831 Introduction, in Butler, *Frankenstein*, p. 196.
5. 1831 Introduction, in Butler, *Frankenstein*, p. 192.
6. Anne K. Mellor, *Mary Shelley: Her Life, Her Fiction, Her Monsters*. New York: Methuen, 1988, p. 57.
7. Quoted in Mellor, *Mary Shelley*, pp. 9–10.
8. Godwin ran his own small publishing house and released her volume under the imprint of the "Godwin Juvenile Library." By 1812, when Mary was fifteen, the verses had sold well enough to require four editions; they were reissued once more in 1830 with illustrations by the noted artist Robert Cruikshank.
9. Quoted in Maurice Hindle, ed., *Frankenstein or the Modern Prometheus*. New York: Penguin Books, 1985, pp. 14–15.
10. Quoted in Mellor, *Mary Shelley*, p. 32.
11. 1831 Introduction, in Butler, *Frankenstein*, p. 197.
12. From the Preface to *Frankenstein*, in Hindle, *Frankenstein*, pp. 61–62.

13. For these and other changes Shelley made in the manuscript, see Mellor, *Mary Shelley*, pp. 59–63.
14. Quoted in Donald F. Glut, *The Frankenstein Legend: A Tribute to Mary Shelley and Boris Karloff.* Metuchen, NJ: Scarecrow Press, 1973, p. 24.
15. Quoted in Muriel Spark, *Mary Shelley.* New York: Dutton, 1987, p. 154.
16. Quoted in Glut, *The Frankenstein Legend*, pp. 24–25.
17. Quoted in Spark, *Mary Shelley*, p. 154.
18. Elizabeth Nitchie, *Mary Shelley, Author of* Frankenstein. Westport, CT: Greenwood Press, 1970, pp. 147–48.
19. R.E. Dowse and D.J. Palmer, eds., *Frankenstein or the Modern Prometheus.* New York: Dutton, 1963, p. xii.
20. Quoted in Spark, *Mary Shelley*, p. 57.
21. Quoted in Emily W. Sunstein, *Mary Shelley: Romance and Reality.* Boston: Little, Brown, 1989, p. 223.
22. Quoted in Mellor, *Mary Shelley*, p. 147.
23. Mellor, *Mary Shelley*, pp. 147–48.
24. Spark, *Mary Shelley*, p. 154.

CHAPTER 1

The Story, Its Conception, and the Sources of Its Ideas

READINGS ON
FRANKENSTEIN

The Story of *Frankenstein*

Leslie Halliwell

People who know *Frankenstein* only from the movies are often surprised to learn that in Mary Shelley's novel the so-called Monster is a thinking, talking being whose predicament evokes considerable sympathy. This concise overview, crafted by the noted film historian Leslie Halliwell, effectively brings the story to life by interspersing brief but highly appropriate and descriptive passages from the novel.

The novel opens strikingly enough as Victor Frankenstein . . . pursues across the frozen ice, north of Archangel, a strange misshapen giant of a man. The figure disappears among the icebergs. To the British explorer [Captain Robert Walton] who saves him, our exhausted hero tells a strange story:

At the University of Ingolstadt, Frankenstein, the scion [heir] of a noble family, had studied alchemy [an ancient art that used magic elixers and formulas] as well as modern science, and gradually became obsessed with the hope that he might discover the elixir of life. After nights of near-madness spent in the examination of bodily decay in charnel houses, he became convinced that the great secret resided in the ultraviolet ray, electrically transmitted. His more advanced studies involved vivisection [dissecting bodies], grave robbing, and the stealing of remains from slaughter houses; and from the parts thus assembled he created an eight-foot giant in human form.

> One of the phenomena which had peculiarly attracted my attention was the structure of the human frame, and, indeed, any animal endued with life. Whence, I often asked myself, did the principle of life proceed? It was a bold question, and one which has ever been considered as a mystery; yet with how many things are we upon the brink of becoming acquainted, if cowardice or carelessness did not restrain our inquiries. . . . I beheld the corruption of death succeed to the blooming cheek of life; I saw how the worm inherited the

wonders of the eye and brain. I paused, examining and analysing . . . the change from life to death, and death to life, until from the midst of this darkness a sudden light broke in upon me—a light so brilliant and wondrous, yet so simple, that while I became dizzy with the immensity of the prospect which it illustrated, I was surprised, that among so many men of genius who had directed their inquiries towards the same science, that I alone should be reserved to discover so astonishing a secret. . . .

I collected bones from charnel houses; and disturbed, with profane fingers, the tremendous secrets of the human frame. In a solitary chamber, or rather cell, at the top of the house, and separated from all the other apartments by a gallery and staircase, I kept my workshop of filthy creation: my eye-balls were starting from their sockets in attending to the details of my employment. The dissecting room and the slaughter house furnished many of my materials; and often did my human nature turn with loathing from my occupation, whilst, still urged on by an eagerness which perpetually increased, I brought my work near to a conclusion.

It was on a dreary night of November that I beheld the accomplishment of my toils. With an anxiety that almost amounted to agony, I collected the instruments of life around me, that I might infuse a spark of being into the lifeless thing that lay at my feet. It was already one in the morning; the rain pattered dismally against the panes, and my candle was nearly burnt out, when, by the glimmer of the half-extinguished light, I saw the dull yellow eye of the creature open; it breathed hard, and a convulsive motion agitated its limbs. . . .

DISGUSTED BY HIS CREATION

That night, Victor's sleep is filled with horrid dreams, including one of his mother's corpse in her shroud, with 'grave worms crawling in the folds of the flannel':

I started from my sleep with horror; a cold dew covered my forehead, my teeth chattered, and every limb became convulsed: when, by the dim and yellow light of the moon, as it forced its way through the window shutters, I beheld the wretch—the miserable monster whom I had created. He held up the curtain of the bed; and his eyes, if eyes they may be called, were fixed on me. His jaw opened, and he muttered some inarticulate sounds, while a grin wrinkled his cheeks. He might have spoken, but I did not hear it; one hand was stretched out, seemingly to detain me, but I escaped, and rushed down stairs. I took refuge in the courtyard belonging to the house which I inhabited; where I remained during the rest of the night, walking up and down in the greatest agitation, listening attentively, catching and fearing each sound as if it were to announce the approach of the demoniacal corpse to which I had so miserably given life.

... Victor thus deserts his creation, and suffers for months from remorse and from physical revulsion at having created it. The creature disappears entirely. Then Victor has word from home that his younger brother has been foully murdered, and near the end of his hasty journey to comfort his family he sees on the hillside something which makes him cringe with guilt . . .

> I perceived in the gloom a figure which stole from behind a clump of trees near me; I stood fixed, gazing intently: I could not be mistaken. A flash of lightning illuminated the object, and discovered its shape plainly to me; its gigantic stature, and the deformity of its aspect, more hideous than belongs to humanity, instantly informed me that it was the wretch, the filthy demon, to whom I had given life. What did he there? Could he be (I shuddered at the conception) the murderer of my brother? No sooner did that idea cross my imagination, than I became convinced of its truth. . . .

VICTOR CONFRONTS THE MONSTER

When he arrives home, Victor discovers that a servant girl, Justine, is suspected of the murder. He knows her to be innocent: Justine, however, is caught and hanged, which naturally aggravates Victor's guilt complex. Later, on a glacier below Mont Blanc

> . . . I suddenly beheld the figure of a man, at some distance, advancing towards me with superhuman speed. He bounded over the crevices in the ice, among which I had walked with caution; his stature, also, as he approached, seemed to exceed that of man. . . . I perceived, as the shape came nearer (sight tremendous and abhorred!) that it was the wretch whom I had created . . .
>
> 'Devil,' I exclaimed, 'do you dare approach me? and do not you fear the fierce vengeance of my arm wreaked on your miserable head? Begone, vile insect! or rather, stay, that I may trample you to dust! and, oh! that I could, with the extinction of your miserable existence, restore those victims whom you have so diabolically murdered!'
>
> 'I expected this reception,' said the demon. 'All men hate the wretched; how, then, must I be hated, who am miserable beyond all living things! Yet you, my creator, detest and spurn me, thy creature, to whom thou art bound by ties only dissoluble by the annihilation of one of us. You purpose to kill me. How dare you sport thus with life? Do your duty towards me, and I will do mine towards you and the rest of mankind. If you will comply with my conditions, I will leave them and you at peace; but if you refuse, I will glut the maw of death, until it be satiated with the blood of your remaining friends.'

'Abhorred monster! fiend that thou art! the tortures of hell are too mild a vengeance for thy crimes Wretched devil! . . . Begone! I will not hear you. There can be no community between you and me; we are enemies. Begone, or let us try our strength in a fight, in which one must fall.'

[The Monster tells Victor about his first sensations on awakening into the world.] He goes on to describe at great length how he stayed with a blind man who could not see his ugliness. . . . Finally he tells how he came upon the small boy and murdered him because he was of the Frankenstein family. . . .

> The being finished speaking, and fixed his looks upon me in expectation of a reply. But I was bewildered, perplexed, and unable to arrange my ideas sufficiently to understand the full extent of his proposition. He continued —
>
> 'You must create a female for me, with whom I can live in the interchange of those sympathies necessary for my being. This you alone can do; and I demand it of you as a right which you must not refuse to concede.' . . .
>
> 'I do refuse it,' I replied; 'and no torture shall ever extort a consent from me. You may render me the most miserable of men, but you shall never make me base in my own eyes. Shall I create another like yourself, whose joint wickedness might desolate the world! Begone! I have answered you; you may torture me, but I will never consent.'

HOUNDED BY THE HIDEOUS FIGURE

Frankenstein has plenty of thinking to do. Eventually he retreats from the society he knows and sets up a new laboratory in a remote part of the Orkneys. Here under the crudest conditions, and despite his initial horror at the idea, he prepares to build a bride for the monster. The original creature, however, is so impatient that the pair of them fall out, and Frankenstein sets out once more on his desperate travels.

But there is no escape for poor Victor. The monster next murders his friend Henry, and Victor is imprisoned for three months before his innocence is established. Then at last he marries his [fiancée] Elizabeth and sets off to honeymoon in Evian. But he should have heeded the monster's warning of further revenge to come. The honeymoon night is a tragic one.

> She left me, and I continued some time walking up and down the passages of the house, and inspecting every corner that might afford a retreat to my adversary. But I discovered no trace of him, and was beginning to conjecture that some fortunate chance had intervened to prevent the execution of his menaces, when suddenly I heard a shrill and dreadful scream. It came from the room into which Elizabeth had re-

tired. . . . She was there, lifeless and inanimate, thrown across the bed, her head hanging down, and her pale and distorted features half covered by her hair. . . .

While I still hung over her in the agony of despair, I happened to look up. The windows of the room had before been darkened, and I felt a kind of panic on seeing the pale yellow light of the moon illuminate the chamber. The shutters had been thrown back; and, with a sensation of horror not to be described, I saw at the open window a figure the most hideous and abhorred. A grin was on the face of the monster; he seemed to jeer as with his fiendish finger he pointed towards the corpse of my wife. I rushed towards the window and, drawing a pistol from my bosom, fired; but he eluded me, leaped from his station, and running with the swiftness of lightning, plunged into the lake.

. . . When Victor sets out on more rather aimless wanderings in pursuit of his demon, the novel threatens to turn into a world tour. The Rhône, the Mediterranean, the Black Sea, Tartary, Russia are all explored in vain. But sometimes the monster taunts Victor with clues and messages, and one of these sets him on a new tack: 'My reign is not yet over. You live, and my power is complete. Follow me: I seek the everlasting ices of the north, where you will feel the misery of cold and frost to which I am impassive. You will find near this place, if you follow not too tardily, a dead hare: eat, and be refreshed. Come on, my enemy: we have yet to wrestle for our lives: but many hard and miserable hours must you endure until that period shall arrive.' Victor follows the trail across the Arctic ocean until his dogs die one by one and, as we have seen, he is rescued [by Captain Walton] half dead to tell his story. The monster eludes him still.

Oh! when will my guiding spirit, in conducting me to the demon, allow me the rest I so much desire; or must I die and yet he live? If I do, swear to me, Walton, that he shall not escape; that you will seek him and satisfy my vengeance in his death. . . . If he should appear; if the ministers of vengeance should conduct him to you, swear that he shall not live—swear that he shall not triumph over my accumulated woes, and survive to add to the list of his dark crimes. . . .

THE MONSTER'S LONELY FATE

After several days Victor dies, and in a letter home his rescuer adds a footnote:

Great God! what a scene has just taken place! I am yet dizzy with the remembrance of it. I hardly know whether I shall have the power to detail it; yet the tale which I have recorded would be incomplete without this final and wonderful catastrophe.

I entered the cabin where lay the remains of my ill-fated and admirable friend. Over him hung a form which I cannot find words to describe; gigantic in stature, yet uncouth and distorted in its proportions. . . .

He paused, looking on me with wonder; and, again turning towards the lifeless form of his creator, he seemed to forget my presence, and every feature and gesture seemed instigated by the wildest rage of some uncontrollable passion.

'That is also my victim!' he exclaimed: 'in his murder my crimes are consummated; the miserable series of my being is wound to its close! Oh, Frankenstein! generous and self-devoted being! what does it avail that I now ask thee to pardon me? I, who irretrievably destroyed thee by destroying all thou lovedst. Alas! he is cold, he cannot answer me.' . . .

'Once my fancy was soothed with dreams of virtue, of fame, and of enjoyment. Once I falsely hoped to meet with beings who, pardoning my outward form, would love me for the excellent qualities which I was capable of unfolding. I was nourished with high thoughts of honour and devotion. But now crime has degraded me beneath the meanest animal. No guilt, no mischief, no malignity, no misery, can be found comparable to mine. When I run over the frightful catalogue of my sins, I cannot believe that I am the same creature whose thoughts were once filled with sublime and transcendent visions of the beauty and the majesty of goodness. But it is even so; the fallen angel becomes a malignant devil. Yet even that enemy of God and man had friends and associates in his desolation; I am alone . . .'

'Fear not that I shall be the instrument of future mischief. My work is nearly complete. Neither yours nor any man's death is needed to consummate the series of my being, and accomplish that which must be done; but it requires my own. . . . I shall die. I shall no longer feel the agonies which now consume me, or be the prey of feelings unsatisfied, yet unquenched. He is dead who called me into being; and when I shall be no more the very remembrance of us both will speedily vanish.'. . .

'Farewell! I leave you, and in you the last of human kind whom these eyes will ever behold. Farewell, Frankenstein!'. . .

'My spirit will sleep in peace; or if it thinks, it will not surely think thus. Farewell.'

He sprung from the cabin window, as he said this, upon the ice-raft which lay close to the vessel. He was soon borne away by the waves and lost in darkness and distance.

How the Author Conceived the Basic Premise

Mary Shelley

No writer has ever explained the original conception of the kernel of the Frankenstein story better than Mary Shelley herself. The book was first published anonymously in 1818; in the years that followed, after she was revealed as the author, people frequently asked her where she had gotten the main idea, namely that of the reanimation of a corpse. When the book was republished, with some revisions by the author, in October 1831, Mary Shelley provided a special introduction answering this question. That introduction is reprinted below almost in its entirety. It recounts the events of June 1816, when she, then only nineteen, and her soon-to-be husband, the poet Percy Bysshe Shelley, visited the Villa Diodati, near Geneva, Switzerland. There they were the guests of the renowned poet Lord Byron and his friend, Dr. John Polidori. Note the author's references to the controversial eighteenth-century biologist Erasmus Darwin, grandfather of famed naturalist Charles Darwin; and to galvanism, the application of electric currents directly to muscles and other tissues. Her phrase "when I was not alone" near the end of the piece refers to the fact that Percy Shelley drowned in 1822, nine years before she wrote it.

The publishers . . . in selecting *Frankenstein* for one of their series, expressed a wish that I should furnish them with some account of the origin of the story. I am the more willing to comply, because I shall thus give a general answer to the question, so very frequently asked me—'How I, then a young

Adapted from Mary Shelley's Introduction to *Frankenstein, or The Modern Prometheus* (London, 1831).

girl, came to think of and to dilate upon so very hideous an idea?' It is true that I am very averse to bringing myself forward in print; but as my account will only appear as an appendage to a former production, and as it will be confined to such topics as have connexion with my authorship alone, I can scarcely accuse myself of a personal intrusion.

CASTLES IN THE AIR

It is not singular [unusual] that, as the daughter of two persons of distinguished literary celebrity, I should very early in life have thought of writing. As a child I scribbled; and my favourite pastime during the hours given me for recreation was to 'write stories'. Still, I had a dearer pleasure than this, which was the formation of castles in the air—the indulging in waking dreams—the following up trains of thought, which had for their subject the formation of a succession of imaginary incidents. My dreams were at once more fantastic and agreeable than my writings. In the latter I was a close imitator—rather doing as others had done than putting down the suggestions of my own mind. What I wrote was intended at least for one other eye—my childhood's companion and friend [perhaps Isabel Baxter, with whom she stayed in Scotland in her midteens], but my dreams were all my own; I accounted for them to nobody; they were my refuge when annoyed—my dearest pleasure when free.

I lived principally in the country as a girl, and passed a considerable time in Scotland. I made occasional visits to the more picturesque parts; but my habitual residence was on the blank and dreary northern shores of the Tay, near Dundee. Blank and dreary on retrospection I call them; they were not so to me then. They were the . . . pleasant region where unheeded I could commune with the creatures of my fancy. I wrote then—but in a most common-place style. It was beneath the trees of the grounds belonging to our house, or on the bleak sides of the woodless mountains near, that my true compositions, the airy flights of my imagination, were born and fostered. I did not make myself the heroine of my tales. Life appeared to me too common-place an affair as regarded myself. I could not figure to myself that romantic woes or wonderful events would ever be my lot; but I was not confined to my own identity, and I could people the hours with creations far more interesting to me at that age than my own sensations.

After this my life became busier, and reality stood in place of fiction. My husband [Percy Bysshe Shelley], however, was from the first, very anxious that I should prove myself worthy of my parentage, and enrol myself on the page of fame. He was for ever inciting me to obtain literary reputation, which even on my own part I cared for then, though since I have become infinitely indifferent to it. At this time he desired that I should write, not so much with the idea that I could produce any thing worthy of notice, but, that he might himself judge how far I possessed the promise of better things hereafter. Still I did nothing. Travelling, and the cares of a family, occupied my time; and study, in the way of reading or improving my ideas in communication with his far more cultivated mind, was all of literary employment that engaged my attention.

CONJURING UP GHOSTS

In the summer of 1816, we visited Switzerland, and became the neighbours of Lord Byron. At first we spent our pleasant hours on the lake, or wandering on its shores; and Lord Byron, who was writing the third canto of *Childe Harold,* was the only one among us who put his thoughts upon paper. These, as he brought them successively to us, clothed in all the light and harmony of poetry, seemed to stamp as divine the glories of heaven and earth, whose influences we partook with him.

But it proved a wet, ungenial summer, and incessant rain often confined us for days to the house. Some volumes of ghost stories, translated from the German into French, fell into our hands. There was the *History of the Inconstant Lover,* who, when he thought to clasp the bride to whom he had pledged his vows, found himself in the arms of the pale ghost of her whom he had deserted. There was the tale of the sinful founder of his race [a vampire story] whose miserable doom it was to bestow the kiss of death on all the younger sons of his fated house, just when they reached the age of promise. His gigantic, shadowy form, clothed like the ghost in *Hamlet,* in complete armour, but with the beaver up, was seen at midnight, by the moon's fitful beams, to advance slowly along the gloomy avenue. The shape was lost beneath the shadow of the castle walls; but soon a gate swung back, a step was heard, the door of the chamber opened, and he advanced to the couch of the blooming youths, cradled in healthy sleep. Eternal sorrow sat upon his face as he bent down and kissed the forehead of the boys, who from that hour withered like flowers snapt upon the stalk. I have not seen these stories since then; but their incidents are as fresh in my mind as if I had read them yesterday.

'We will each write a ghost story', said Lord Byron; and his proposition was acceded to. There were four of us. The noble author began a tale. . . . Shelley, more apt to embody ideas and sentiments in the radiance of brilliant imagery, and in the music of the most melodious verse that adorns our language, than to invent the machinery of a story, commenced one founded on the experiences of his early life. Poor Polidori had some terrible idea about a skull-headed lady who was so punished for peeping through a keyhole—what to see I forget—something very shocking and wrong of course; but when she was reduced to a worse condition than the renowned Tom of Coventry ["peeping Tom," who was supposedly struck blind for spying the naked Lady Godiva], he did not know what to do with her and was obliged to dispatch her to the tomb of the Capulets, the only place for which she was fitted. The illustrious poets also, annoyed by the platitude of prose, speedily relinquished their uncongenial task.

MARY SEARCHES FOR A STORY

I busied myself *to think of a story,*—a story to rival those which had excited us to this task. One which would speak to the mysterious fears of our nature and awaken thrilling horror—one to make the reader dread to look round, to curdle the blood, and quicken the beatings of the heart. If I did not accomplish these things, my ghost story would be unworthy of its name. I thought and pondered—vainly. I felt that blank incapability of invention which is the greatest misery of authorship, when dull Nothing replies to our anxious invocations. 'Have you thought of a story?' I was asked each morning, and each morning I was forced to reply with a mortifying negative.

Every thing must have a beginning . . . and that beginning must be linked to something that went before. The Hindoos [Hindus] give the world an elephant to support it, but they make the elephant stand upon a tortoise. Invention, it must be humbly admitted, does not consist in creating out of void, but out of chaos; the materials must, in the first place, be afforded: it can give form to dark, shapeless substances, but cannot bring into being the substance itself. In all matters of discovery and invention, even of those that appertain to the imagination, we are continually reminded of the story of

Columbus and his egg. [When a Spanish courtier told Columbus that anyone could have discovered the West Indies, he challenged the person to make an egg stand on end. When the person failed, Columbus managed the trick by crushing one end.] Invention consists in the capacity of seizing on the capabilities of a subject: and in the power of moulding and fashioning ideas suggested to it.

Many and long were the conversations between Lord Byron and Shelley, to which I was a devout but nearly silent listener. During one of these, various philosophical doctrines were discussed and among others the nature of the principle of life, and whether there was any probability of its ever being discovered and communicated. They talked of the experiments of Dr Darwin (I speak not of what the Doctor really did, or said that he did, but, as more to my purpose, of what was then spo-

---

HOLLYWOOD RE-CREATES THE VILLA DIODATI

This is an excerpt from the screenplay (by John L. Balderston and William Hurlbut) of the 1935 film Bride of Frankenstein. *The filmmakers placed the Shelleys and Lord Byron in the Villa Diodati in an imaginary scene reminiscent of the one that actually inspired the concept for the novel (the difference being that here the novel has supposedly already been written).*

MARY, SHELLEY AND BYRON . . . MED. THREE-SHOT

Even Shelley is brought out of his concentration to smile at his friend's fancy.

BYRON: Come, Mary—come and watch the storm.

He holds out his hand to her.

CUT TO

MARY . . . CLOSE UP

MARY: *(always demure, gently poised and mild)*
You know how lightning alarms me.

She chooses another skein of silks ready to thread her needle. There is a flash of lightning and crash of thunder.

I am trying not to hear the horrid thunder—or to see the lightnings. Shelley, darling, will you please turn up the lamps a little more?

BYRON . . . CLOSE UP

He has been regarding her during this.

BYRON: Astonishing creature . . .

CUT TO

ken of as having been done by him), who preserved a piece of vermicelli in a glass case, till by some extraordinary means it began to move with voluntary motion. Not thus, after all, would life be given. Perhaps a corpse would be reanimated; galvanism had given token of such things: perhaps the component parts of a creature might be manufactured, brought together, and endued with vital warmth.

IN A MOONLIT ROOM

Night waned upon this talk, and even the witching hour had gone by, before we retired to rest. When I placed my head on my pillow, I did not sleep, nor could I be said to think. My imagination, unbidden, possessed and guided me, gifting the successive images that arose in my mind with a vividness far beyond the usual bounds of reverie. I saw—with shut eyes,

---

MARY . . . CLOSE UP

  MARY: I, Lord Byron?

CUT TO

MARY, SHELLEY AND BYRON . . . MED. SHOT

  BYRON: Frightened of thunder—fearful of the dark—and yet
    you have written a tale that sent my blood into icy creeps.

CUT TO

MARY . . . CLOSE UP

She chuckles a little smile, but is centred upon threading her needle.

CUT TO

MARY, SHELLEY AND BYRON . . . MED. SHOT

  BYRON: Look at her, Shelley, can you believe that bland and
    lovely brow conceived a Frankenstein—a monster created
    from the cadavers out of rifled graves.—Isn't it astonishing?

CUT TO

MARY AND BYRON . . . MED. TWO-SHOT. . . .

  BYRON: No wonder Murray has refused to publish the book—
    says their reading public would be *too* shocked.

CUT TO

MARY . . . CLOSE UP

  MARY: *(in her mild, calm voice)*
  It will be published, I think.

Quoted in Leslie Halliwell, *The Dead That Walk: Dracula, Frankenstein, the Mummy, and Other Favorite Movie Monsters.* New York: Continuum, 1986, pp.131–32.

but acute mental vision—I saw the pale student of unhallowed arts kneeling beside the thing he had put together. I
saw the hideous phantasm of a man stretched out, and then,
on the working of some powerful engine, show signs of life,
and stir with an uneasy, half-vital motion. Frightful must it
be; for supremely frightful would be the effect of any human
endeavour to mock the stupendous mechanism of the Creator of the world. His success would terrify the artist; he
would rush away from his odious [disgusting] handywork,
horror-stricken. He would hope that, left to itself, the slight
spark of life which he had communicated would fade; that
this thing, which had received such imperfect animation
would subside into dead matter; and he might sleep in the
belief that the silence of the grave would quench forever the
transient existence of the hideous corpse which he had
looked upon as the cradle of life. He sleeps; but he is awak-
ened; he opens his eyes; behold, the horrid thing stands at his
bedside, opening his curtains and looking on him with yellow, watery, but speculative eyes.

I opened mine in terror. The idea so possessed my mind,
that a thrill of fear ran through me, and I wished to exchange
the ghastly image of my fancy for the realities around. I see
them still; the very room . . . the closed shutters, with the
moonlight struggling through, and the sense I had that the
glassy lake and white high Alps were beyond. I could not so
easily get rid of my hideous phantom; still it haunted me. I
must try to think of something else. I recurred to my ghost
story—my tiresome, unlucky ghost story! O! if I could only
contrive one which would frighten my reader as I myself had
been frightened that night!

Swift as light and as cheering was the idea that broke in
upon me. 'I have found it! What terrified me will terrify others; and I need only describe the spectre which had haunted
my midnight pillow.' On the morrow I announced that I had
thought of a story. I began that day with the words, 'It was on
a dreary night of November,' making only a transcript of the
grim terrors of my waking dream.

"MY HIDEOUS PROGENY"

At first I thought but a few pages—of a short tale; but Shelley
urged me to develope the idea at greater length. I certainly did
not owe the suggestion of one incident, nor scarcely of one
train of feeling, to my husband, and yet but for his incitement

it would never have taken the form in which it was presented to the world. From this declaration I must except the preface. As far as I can recollect, it was entirely written by him.

And now, once again, I bid my hideous progeny [offspring] go forth and prosper. I have affection for it, for it was the offspring of happy days, when death and grief were but words, which found no true echo in my heart. Its several pages speak of many a walk, many a drive, and many a conversation, when I was not alone; and my companion was one who, in this world, I shall never see more. But this is for myself; my readers have nothing to do with these associations.

I will add but one word as to the alterations I have made. They are principally those of style. I have changed no portion of the story nor introduced any new ideas or circumstances. I have mended the language where it was so bald as to interfere with the interest of the narrative; and these changes occur almost exclusively in the beginning of the first volume. Throughout they are entirely confined to such parts as are mere adjuncts to the story, leaving the core and substance of it untouched.

Frankenstein's Exploitation of the Prometheus Myths

M.K. Joseph

The Greek myths of Prometheus, one of an early race of gods called Titans, fascinated Mary and Percy Shelley and their poet friend Lord Byron. One of these tales told of Prometheus *plasticator*, or molder, who fashioned humans from clay; the other of Prometheus *pyrphoros*, or fire-wielder, who gave knowledge of fire to humans. As M.K. Joseph, a former professor at the University of Auckland, New Zealand, explains here, Mary Shelley effectively wove both of these themes into the fabric of her novel *Frankenstein*. In a way, then, Victor Frankenstein is a "modern Prometheus" (the book's subtitle), infusing the spark of life into nonliving matter.

When Mary Wollstonecraft Godwin began to write *Frankenstein*, she was not quite nineteen; yet none of her later novels has achieved anything like the same universal hold on the imagination. Whatever she may have owed to other novelists, particularly to her father William Godwin and to the American Charles Brockden Brown, the novel remains completely original. In spite of her errors, which are those of a novice—particularly her tendency to invent fresh improbabilities rather than to think her way through difficult passages in the story—the central idea is carried through with considerable skill and force.

The unexpected and bizarre success of the novel was due to one of those lucky accidents which, in most writers' lives, happen only once. For two troubled and uncertain years, she had been living with [poet Percy Bysshe] Shelley. Now, in the summer of 1816, they had temporarily escaped from England and were settled in Geneva, among the splendours of lake

Excerpted from the Introduction to *Frankenstein, or The Modern Prometheus*, by Mary Shelley, edited by M.K. Joseph. Copyright © 1969 by·Oxford University Press. Reprinted by permission of the publisher.

and mountains, and in the stimulating company of [poet Lord] Byron. The germ of *Frankenstein* is to be found somewhere in their wide-ranging nightly conversations, which must have covered, not only gothic terrors and galvanism and current theories on the origin of life, but also the myth of Prometheus and its significance. For Mary subtitled her story 'the modern Prometheus', and this is an essential clue to its meaning.

AN ANCIENT MYTH LINKED TO MODERN SCIENCE

The myth of Prometheus contained two main elements. The first, best known through the *Prometheus Bound* of [the fifth-century B.C. Greek playwright] Aeschylus, was the story of Prometheus *pyrphoros*, who had brought down fire from the sun in order to succour mankind, and whom [the chief god] Zeus had punished by chaining him to the Caucasus [a mountain chain] with an eagle feeding on his vitals. The second was the story of Prometheus *plasticator* who, in some versions, was said to have created or recreated mankind by animating a figure made of clay. This aspect of the myth, little used by the Greeks and unknown to Aeschylus or Hesiod, seems to have been more popular with the Romans.

By about the second or third century A.D., the two elements were fused together, so that the fire stolen by Prometheus was also the fire of life with which he animated his man of clay. This gave a radically new significance to the myth . . . with Prometheus as the demiurge or deputy creator, but which could also be readily allegorized by Christians and was frequently used in the Middle Ages as a representation of the creative power of God. By the Renaissance, the image was a familiar one, as in Othello's words over Desdemona [in Shakespeare's *Othello*]:

> . . . I know not where is that Promethean heat
>   That can thy light relume.

Later still, Prometheus became an accepted image of the creative artist. . . .

Before 1816 [Percy] Shelley seems to have been unaware of the potent symbolic significance of the myth; it was Byron, to whom Prometheus had been a familiar figure ever since he translated a portion of Aeschylus while still a schoolboy . . . who opened his eyes to its potentialities during that summer at Geneva. That it was discussed at the time can be inferred from the results: Byron's poem, 'Prometheus', written in July 1816; his *Manfred*, with its Promethean hero, begun in September; and Shelley's *Prometheus Unbound*, in part a reply to *Manfred*, begun later in 1818. But Mary Shelley was first in the field with her 'modern Prometheus', and she alone seized

---

PROMETHEUS: FATHER OF THE HUMAN RACE

In this excerpt from his book Myths and Their Meanings, *literary scholar Max J. Herzberg briefly summarizes the* Prometheus *myths.*

For a time Prometheus was the chosen counselor of Jupiter, who relied upon him for help in all things. Yet between them in time a quarrel arose; and all because of mankind. For when Jupiter beheld how men fell away from their former glory in the Silver Age, he swept them off the face of the earth, and resolved to create a new race. He called upon Prometheus for assistance, and the Titan took clay from the banks of a river in Arcadia and molded it into the likeness of the gods and breathed the breath of life into the images that he made. So a new race was born.

Yet these men were feebler than the men of the two preceding ages, and they came into a world that demanded more of them than had ever before been demanded of men. They had to struggle against the changes of the weather. The earth would not bear food for them unless they first tilled the soil, and around them were dangerous wild beasts. It seemed as if this race would perish unless help came.

Prometheus, looking down upon them, saw what was happening.

"Come," he said to Jupiter, "let us give these poor creatures the blessed gift of fire. With fire they will not need to fear the cold. With fire they can make themselves tools and weapons."

But Jupiter feared that if he gave this great boon to men, they would think themselves the equals of the gods, and he refused to grant the request of Prometheus. The Titan was deeply grieved, and at length he resolved that he would no longer dwell with Jupiter but would make his abode with men. So he left Olympus, and carried with him, hidden in a reed, the gift of fire. Prometheus taught men how with fire they might make weapons to fight wild beasts and to contend with their enemies, how with fire they might contrive tools for all handicrafts and trades.

Max J. Herzberg, *Myths and Their Meanings*. Boston: Allyn and Bacon, n.d., pp. 14–15.

on the vital significance of making Prometheus the creator rather than, as in Byron and Shelley, the suffering champion of mankind. In doing so, she linked the myth with certain current scientific theories which suggested that the 'divine spark' of life might be electrical or quasi-electrical in nature.

ELECTRICITY THE DIVINE FIRE

In the novel itself, Victor Frankenstein is understandably reluctant to reveal how he gave life to his creature; but there are clues to what Mary Shelley had in mind. In her Introduction she recalls the talk about [eighteenth-century biologist] Erasmus Darwin, who had 'preserved a piece of vermicelli in a glass case, till by some extraordinary means it began to move with voluntary motion'; but this sounds like an ordinary case of alleged spontaneous generation. 'Not thus, after all, would life be given. Perhaps a corpse would be re-animated; galvanism [application of electricity to muscles and other tissues] had given token of such things: perhaps the component parts of a creature might be manufactured, brought together, and endued with vital warmth.' She then goes on to describe the half-waking reverie which gave her the beginning of her story, in which 'I saw the hideous phantasm of a man stretched out, and then, on the working of some powerful engine, show signs of life, and stir with an uneasy, half vital motion.' Nor is the story itself without hints: in Chapter II a discourse on electricity and magnetism—the point is more explicit in *1818*—turns Frankenstein's mind away from alchemy [an ancient art dealing with magic elixers]; and in Chapter V the 'instruments of life' which Frankenstein assembles before infusing the 'spark of life' also suggest an electrical rather than a biological process.

Frankenstein's change of interest from alchemy to chemistry and electricity is a circumstance obviously drawn from Shelley himself; and with the mention of electricity as vitalizing force we come . . . to a central idea of Shelley's which was to emerge, a little later, in the last act of *Prometheus Unbound*. In his eclectic synthesis of ideas drawn from [the well-known scientists] Newton, Volta, Galvani, Erasmus Darwin, and Humphry Davy (whom Mary was reading in October 1816), electricity became the divine fire, the life-principle, and the physical manifestation of spiritual love. . . . It seems likely that, during the conversations at Diodati [Byron's villa near Geneva], Mary absorbed from Shelley—and perhaps from Polidori [Byron's doctor friend] as well—the idea of making electricity the animating force, the scientific equivalent of that divine spark which, in the myth, Prometheus had stolen from the sun. . . .

IS SCIENCE CREATIVE?

The implications of Mary Shelley's 'ghost-story' go much further than she or any of her circle seem to have understood. . . . With unassuming originality, her 'modern Prometheus' challenges the whole myth of . . . the artist as Promethean creator. One of its themes is solitude—the solitude of one who turns his back on his kind in his obsessive pursuit of the secrets of nature. Frankenstein sins against the . . . ideal of social benevolence. . . .

Prometheus was also an accepted metaphor of the artist, but when Mary Shelley transfers this to the scientist, the implications are radical. If Frankenstein, as scientist, is 'the modern Prometheus', then science too is creative; but whereas the world of art is ideal and speculative, that of science is real and inescapable. It must then take the consequences: the scientist, himself a creature, has taken on the role and burden of a creator. If Frankenstein corrupts the monster by his rejection . . . we are left asking a question which demands another kind of answer: what has rejected and corrupted Frankenstein? [God perhaps?] And if Prometheus, in the romantic tradition, is identified with human revolt, is the monster what that revolt looks like from the other side—a pitiful botched-up creature, a 'filthy mass that moved and talked', which brings nothing but grief and destruction upon the power that made him?

Mary Shelley wrote in the infancy of modern science, when its enormous possibilities were just beginning to be foreseen by imaginative writers like Byron and Shelley and by speculative scientists like Davy and Erasmus Darwin. At the age of nineteen, she achieved the quietly astonishing feat of looking beyond them and creating a lasting symbol of the perils of scientific Prometheanism.

The Monster Modeled on Milton's Adam

Christopher Small

In 1667, the great English poet John Milton (1608–1674) published his masterpiece, the epic poem *Paradise Lost*. Its sweeping verses told the timeless tale of how Satan got Adam and Eve to commit the first sin, a transgression for which God expelled them from the Garden of Eden. In writing *Frankenstein*, Mary Shelley recognized that the man Victor Franken-stein creates has much in common with Milton's Adam, both innocent beings who wake up in a strange world they do not understand and must learn to survive and cope by trial and error. Thus, it is no accident that Shelley's Monster, in attempting to edu-cate himself, reads Milton's *Paradise Lost* and recog-nizes in Adam's situation and predicaments several similarities to his own. This intriguing essay exploring those similarities is from *Mary Shelley's* Frankenstein: *Tracing the Myth*, by noted literary editor and drama critic Christopher Small.

The epigraph to the original edition of *Frankenstein* was taken from Book X of *Paradise Lost*; Adam's expostulation to God:

> Did I request thee, Maker, from my clay
> To mould me Man, did I solicit thee
> From darkness to promote me—?

NO MAKER TO INSTRUCT HIM

The Monster is thus identified from the start, it seems, with Milton's Adam, a bad copy of the first man—although, as Frankenstein says, he, like God, "had selected his features as beautiful". The result is quite different, but clearly related to the original: instead of "fair large Front and Eye sublime", the Monster's "yellow skin scarcely covered the work of muscles

Excerpted from *Mary Shelley's* Frankenstein: *Tracing the Myth*, by Christopher Small (Pittsburgh: University of Pittsburgh Press, 1973). Copyright © 1972 by Christopher Small. Reprinted by permission of the original publisher, Victor Gollancz Ltd., London.

and arteries beneath"; his hair, "of a lustrous black, and flowing", might be like Adam's "hyacinthine locks", his teeth "of
a pearly whiteness" but "these luxuriances only formed a
more horrid contrast with his watery eyes . . . his shrivelled
complexion and straight black lips". The same distorted
equivalence continues when the Monster, in his glacier
meeting with Frankenstein, gives like Adam an account of
his first awakening: apologising in advance and in almost exactly the same terms, for the uncertainty of his memory: "'It
is with considerable difficulty that I remember the original
era of my being: all the events of that period appear confused
and indistinct.'" (As Adam explains to Raphael, "For Man to
tell how human Life began/ Is hard; for who himself beginning knew?")

But instead of coming to life in the unsullied environment
of Eden, where "all things smiled", the Monster wakes in a
charnel-house and finds even his first sensations painful, the
darkness troubling, the light oppressive, hunger and thirst a
torment. The world into which he wanders, though it affords
some of the same facilities as Paradise ("'I ate some berries
which I found hanging on the trees, or lying on the ground. I
slaked my thirst at the brook'") is for the most part unpleasant and bewildering. Without his maker to instruct him as
God instructs Adam he understands nothing and, a crucial
difference, has no God-given language. In Adam's case,
though "who I was, or where, or from what cause" he does
not know, he has only to attempt speech "and forthwith
spake", naming everything in sight. In the Monster's,
Frankenstein has already described his apparition at the bedside, how he could only mutter "inarticulate sounds", although trying to communicate. He does not know the name
of anything, and can hardly be said to think ("'No distinct
ideas occupied my mind; all was confused'"). When he
comes in contact for any length of time with human beings
(the family in the cottage next to which he hides himself) he
doesn't know what they are saying and has to teach himself
language by careful listening; with the fortunate circumstance, it is true, that one of the cottagers is herself learning
from another. The whole cottage episode is in fact inserted in
order that the Monster should learn speech, letters, and the
rudiments of human culture *without being taught*, either by
a human or a divine agency: nothing, and it is essential to the
story that it should so be, is allowed to break his isolation.

TAPPING THE INNATE HUMAN POTENTIAL

Much of this business is simply in accordance with the principle already mentioned, that events however extraordinary should have a "natural" explanation. But Mary's adherence to this rule was less the negative one, of excluding "supernatural" mechanisms by no matter what improbabilities, than the positive one of "delineating . . . human passions", as Shelley said, according to "the elementary principles of human nature". It was necessary for her plot that the Monster should learn to speak and read; but it was necessary much more fundamentally for her purpose that he should do so without a teacher.

One can see at work here the speculation, much indulged in by men of Enlightenment, what would be the effects upon a human being of complete severance from human society from infancy: would a child thus cut off learn to talk at all, would he speak . . . the "language of our first parents", what would his behaviour be? Mary's Monster, though, full-grown—or rather a ready-made adult—is in the situation of [a] child, and her answer is the reasonable one, that child or man so deprived of the normal means of learning will be quite inarticulate. But the Monster's education also demonstrates (and here Mary showed her grasp of processes and capabilities which modern learning theory is only now returning to recognise) that even without any of the ordinary, and necessary circumstances of "socialisation", a human being, born or made, has innate potentialities that allow him to make use of them far beyond mechanically rational expectation. The Monster cannot learn speech without hearing others speak, he cannot read without at least indirect instruction, but he has a "natural" aptitude, even though an artificial creature, which enables him to pick up these human accomplishments with extraordinary rapidity. Thought, one may say, was already present in him, though confused, and logical deduction (learning about fire) was possible for him before language, which expresses but does not originate it, was available to him. The Monster's feats of learning are extraordinary, or far-fetched; but seem less so to anyone who seriously thinks (as Mary may well have thought, watching her baby son exploring and learning about his world) what it is for an infant to learn speech, not as one may acquire another language, but as an absolute beginner.

An Ugly Duckling with a Heart

The Monster, however ill-made, has the potentialities of a child, though starting off, like Adam, fully-grown; and one of Mary's more obvious aims was to show, in accordance with quite un-Miltonic views . . . that an Adam without any of the advantages of the original, and without direct inspiration from God or anywhere else except his own nature, was nevertheless capable of happiness and virtue. Though a monstrosity . . . he has an inbuilt affinity with the natural world: even in his wholly unenlightened state, knowing nothing of himself or his surroundings, he feels pleasure at the sight of the rising moon, though he doesn't know what it is; he listens, again with pleasure, to the song of the birds; and he is immediately attracted by the first human beings he sees, though rejected by them.

Like the ethologist's duckling he is primed for attachment; but being a conspicuously Ugly Duckling is spurned from the beginning. His longing for society and "sympathy" and his deprivation of them are main themes of the story, of which more will be said. The point at the moment is the Monster's potentiality as a new, completely uninstructed being who not only shows remarkable resource and intelligence, but has a "feeling heart". He responds at once to the music played by the inhabitants of the cottage, and to the spectacle of their mutual affection; the girl listening to her father was, he says, "'a lovely sight, even to me, poor wretch! who had never beheld aught beautiful before'", and the emotion they show powerfully affects him. The girl weeps and the father smiles on her and comforts her, whereupon the Monster watching from his hiding place feels "'sensations of a peculiar and overpowering nature: they were a mixture of pain and pleasure, such as I had never before experienced, either from hunger or cold, warmth or food'".

He feels them moreover before he can put words to them; it is only later, after learning a collection of nouns and proper names, that he begins to grasp at abstractions: "'I distinguished several other words, without being able as yet to understand or apply them; such as *good, dearest, unhappy'*." He grows, though still in hiding, to "love and reverence" his "protectors", as, pathetically, "'in an innocent, half-painful self-deceit'", he likes to call them. He is like a lonely child creating an ideal fantasy-family for himself; alternatively, he is in the happy state of pre-lapsarian [before having sinned] Adam: "'My spirits were elevated by the enchanting appearance of nature; the past was blotted from my memory, the present was tranquil, and the future gilded by bright rays of hope and anticipation of joy'."

"MISERY MADE ME A FIEND"

What goes wrong? Superficially, of course, it is simply a matter of bad luck and misunderstanding. The Monster schemes to ingratiate himself with the cottagers by speaking first to the old man who, as well as being gentle and benevolent, is blind and therefore won't know him as a monster. But just when he is about to reveal his identity and throw himself on the old man's mercy, the others return, think that he is attacking their father, and drive him out; shortly afterwards, in fear and disgust they leave the place and the Monster never sees them again. From this time things go from bad to worse for him, he is rejected on all sides, fled from, shot at, and so he becomes by degrees what the others have taken him for, a malignant outcast.

"'I was benevolent and good'," he says to Frankenstein on the glacier; "'misery made me a fiend. Make me happy and I shall again be virtuous'." The same . . . formula appears at other points, and was naturally singled out by Shelley himself as the chief moral of the story: the crimes of the Monster, he said in his first appreciation of the book, were not due to "any unaccountable propensity to evil, but flow irresistibly from certain causes fully adequate to their production . . . Treat a person ill and he will become wicked." Shelley did not inquire why it should be necessary to invent a Monster to demonstrate this—"perhaps the most important and of the most universal application of any moral than can be enforced by example"—nor what the implications were for the character of those who so ill-treated him. . . . He was disinclined to push his analysis so far. For the interdependence of virtue and happiness are only a small part of the moral structure of Frankenstein, which deals in uncertainties much more difficult to resolve than any to be found in [the writings of Mary's father, William] Godwin or, for that matter, in Milton.

THE MONSTER-SATAN

It has already been seen how the Monster, reading *Paradise Lost* and discovering parallels, likens himself not only to

Adam but to Satan: a little later he reverts to this when he finds out that Frankenstein himself had found his own hand- iwork not, as God did, good, but revolting. "'Accursed creator! Why did you form a monster so hideous that even you turned from me in disgust? God, in pity, made man beautiful and al- luring, after his own image; but my form is a filthy type of yours, more horrid even from the very resemblance. Satan had his companions, fellow-devils, to admire and encourage him; but I am solitary and abhorred.'" The Monster is worse off than Adam, exiled from the start, and he is also a Satan, but more wretched than Milton's, who not only had his hell- ish host to support him, described by Milton in such grandiose terms, but was conscious also of belonging in some way, even though a rebel, within God's universe. The Monster belongs nowhere and to nobody. As the story pro- gresses so he becomes progressively more Satanic, his pow- ers growing to positively fiendish capacity (he is alluded to more often as "the Fiend" in the later part of the book) and his ill deeds multiplying accordingly, but also taking on some of the Luciferian majesty so striking in Milton's Satan. In his second confrontation with Frankenstein, in Orkney, he ad- dresses him as "slave"—"'You are my creator, but I am your master'", and threatens him: "'Beware; for I am fearless, and therefore powerful. I will watch with the wiliness of a snake, that I may sting with its venom'." Not surprisingly, Franken- stein in reply calls him simply "Devil".

And at the end, Monster-Adam has become quite explicitly Monster-Satan. He speaks of his last murder and act of re- venge, and says, "'then I was not miserable. I had cast off all feeling, subdued all anguish, to riot in the excess of my de- spair. Evil henceforth became my good.'" ("So farewell Hope, and with Hope farewell Fear, / Farewell Remorse: all Good to me is lost; / Evil be thou my Good," says Milton's Satan.) The Monster is now exactly like Satan remembering his once an- gelic status, but unable to comprehend it: "'I cannot be- lieve,'" he says, "'that I am the same creature whose thoughts were once filled with sublime and transcendant visions of the beauty and majesty of goodness. But it is even so: the fallen angel becomes a malignant devil.'"

Frankenstein Explores the Destructive Potential of Science

Elizabeth Nitchie

In the years directly preceding Mary Shelley's writing of *Frankenstein*, modern scientists had begun to make huge strides toward understanding the workings of nature. Among the scientists whose works she read and was inspired by were English chemist Sir Humphry Davy (1778–1829), who experimented with galvanism, the application of electrical currents to animal tissues; and English biologist Erasmus Darwin, whom she had met as a child when he paid visits to her father. Also influential were her discussions with poets Percy Shelley and Lord Byron (at Diodati, Byron's Swiss villa) about alchemy, the ancient art of conjuring in search of life's secrets, and the potentialities of modern science. She was one of the first modern thinkers to foresee that science, despite its potential to do humanity great good, might also inadvertently unleash destructive forces. She developed this theme so well in her novel that the phrase "to create a Frankenstein" has become a universally recognized description of unexpected and unwanted by-products of science and technology.

No young woman could have written so effectively of Frankenstein's scientific curiosity unless she had shared it to some degree. Absorbing from her reading (she had read [Humphry] Davy in October, 1816, while she was at work on *Frankenstein*) and from the conversation of Shelley some sense of what it meant to think at the same time scientifically and imaginatively, Mary set her lively mind to work on the possible results of research into the mystery of the life principle. It was the discussions at Diodati about the origins

Excerpted from *Mary Shelley: Author of* Frankenstein, by Elizabeth Nitchie. Copyright © 1953 by Rutgers University Press. Reprinted by permission of Rutgers University Press.

of life and the experiments in galvanism that furnished the stimulus for the story of *Frankenstein.* The eager young people gathered in Byron's villa talked of Erasmus Darwin and his reputed success in imparting life to a piece of vermicelli, of his "speculations on the resemblance between the action of the human soul and that of electricity." "Perhaps a corpse would be re-animated; galvanism had given token of such things: perhaps the component parts of a creature might be manufactured, brought together, and endued with vital warmth." Between sleeping and waking one night Mary had a vision of "the pale student of unhallowed arts kneeling beside the thing he had put together," and of his creature. Endowed with life it frightened out of uneasy sleep both its creator and its creator's creator. She had found her "ghost story" to add to the abortive tales the others in the house party had already begun and abandoned. Mary's was to live in successive editions, in allusions, in stage plays, and even in moving pictures (which must "amuse" her in her grave) on through the first half of the twentieth century.

SEARCHING FOR THE SECRET OF LIFE

Victor Frankenstein, the young Genevese student of natural philosophy, felt "the enticements of science," with its "continual food for discovery and wonder," comparing it with other studies in which the student goes only as far as others have gone before him. Always "imbued with a fervent longing to penetrate the secrets of nature," he had his imagination first caught by the alchemists' search for the philosopher's stone and the elixir of life. He read avidly in the works of [medieval alchemists and magicians] Cornelius Agrippa, Albertus Magnus, and Paracelsus. But modern science, as taught by Professor Waldman at Ingolstadt, soon supplanted the ancient magic and put Victor's internal being into a state of turmoil. Waldman's opening lecture on chemistry concluded:

> The ancient teachers of this science promised impossibilities, and performed nothing. The modern masters promise very little; they know that metals cannot be transmuted, and that the elixir of life is a chimera. But these philosophers, whose hands seem only made to dabble in dirt, and their eyes to pore over the microscope or crucible, have indeed performed miracles. They penetrate into the recesses of nature, and show how she works in her hiding places. They ascend into the heavens: they have discovered how the blood circulates,

ERASMUS DARWIN

The distinguished modern literary scholar Leonard Wolf (editor of the widely acclaimed The Annotated Franken- stein*) provides the following information about Erasmus Darwin, one of Mary Shelley's chief scientific influences in writing* Frankenstein *and other works.*

The physician Erasmus Darwin (1731–1802), grandfather of the more famous evolutionist Charles Darwin, was one of the most distinguished scientists of his age. A friend of the Godwin family, Darwin, a zestful womanizer and an audacious stutterer, was capable of dominating any conversation despite his handicap. A corpulent [fat] man, Darwin gave sound advice to his contemporaries on diet. His famous prescription for the disease *pallor et tremor a timore* [literally translated as "pale and shivering in fear"] was "Opium. Wine. Food. Joy."

What is fascinating about Erasmus Darwin is that he was an early friend of Matthew Bolton, who would later become James Watt's partner in the further development of the steam engine, an invention proposed, in fact, some years earlier by Darwin himself. The list of Darwin's friends, most of them members of the Lunar Society (because it met before the full moon in order to save candlepower), reads like a committee of godfathers to the Industrial Revolution: Josiah Wedgwood, potter; James Keir, chemist; James Watt, engineer; Richard Lovell Edgeworth, inventor; and William Small, professor of natural philosophy.

In the Introduction to the 1831 edition of *Frankenstein*, Mary Shelley refers to the "experiments of Dr. Darwin . . . who preserved a piece of vermicelli in a glass case, till by some extraordinary means it began to move with voluntary motion." It is a curious reference, which has been illuminated . . . by . . . Darwin's biographer, Desmond King-Hele, who writes: "Mary Shelley's remarks can, I think, be regarded as recording a mixed-up remembrance by Byron and Shelley of what Darwin wrote in his first note to *The Temple of Nature*. It is entitled 'Spontaneous Vitality of Microscopic animals' . . . Darwin does refer to a 'paste composed of flour and water' in which 'the animalcules called eels' are seen in great abundance and gradually become larger, even in a 'sealed glass phial.' He also refers to the *vorticella* coming to life after being dried. Put this lot together and stir it, and you might arrive at Mary's report."

Leonard Wolf, ed., *The Annotated Frankenstein* (1818 text). New York: Clarkson S. Potter, 1977, pp. 3–4.

and the nature of the air we breathe. They have acquired new and almost unlimited power; they can command the thunders of heaven, mimic the earthquake, and even mock the invisible world with its own shadows.

Guided and advised by Waldman to pursue every branch of natural philosophy, including mathematics, Frankenstein progressed rapidly until he became the equal of his professors. In his interest in the nature and origin of life, he began to study anatomy and physiology. "To examine the causes of life," he concluded, "we must first have recourse to death." In the graveyards and charnel houses he observed the corruption and decay of the human body. "I paused, examining and analyzing all the minutiae of causation, as exemplified in the change from life to death, and death to life until from the midst of this darkness a sudden light broke in upon me. . . . After days and nights of incredible labour and fatigue, I succeeded in discovering the cause of generation and life; nay, more, I became myself capable of bestowing animation upon lifeless matter."

And so Frankenstein, gathering the parts from graves, created his Monster. Finally "on a dreary night in November," he "saw the dull yellow eye of the creature open; it breathed hard, and a convulsive motion agitated its limbs." What the life-giving process was, Mary does not allow Frankenstein to tell us, whether it was galvanism or some chemical change. Her real reasons are obvious; the fictional reasons which she puts into the mouth of the discoverer are the result of his horrible experiences with the "Frankenstein Monster" which he had created and could not control. "I will not lead you on, unguarded and ardent as I then was, to your destruction and infallible misery."

SCIENCE OUT OF CONTROL

The imaginations of later writers were stimulated by *Frankenstein* to use the theme of the creation of life. The Monster is the ancestor of many synthetic human beings and robots. But what is more significant, however questionable the science, Mary had added a useful and pointed phrase to the English vocabulary. In an ironic sense it is easy to apply it to many of the recent inventions and discoveries of man's mind. Frankenstein's motives were not merely the disinterested motives of pure research: he saw himself as the benefactor of the world, creating a new and happy species and even restoring the dead to life. Instead he had created a monstrosity and brought death to the living. We hear almost daily in this Atomic Age the mourning voice of the scientist speaking the words of Frankenstein: "Alas! I had turned loose into the world a depraved wretch, whose delight was in carnage and misery; had he not murdered my brother?" And the creature used for destruction warns: "You are my creator, but I am your master."

CHAPTER 2

Social and Psychological Themes in *Frankenstein*

READINGS ON
FRANKENSTEIN

Society Unfairly Associates Physical Deformity with Monstrosity

Judith Halberstam

Frankenstein illustrates how societal prejudices against physical, or "visual," deformity can automatically categorize a person as bad, inferior, or monstrous, says Judith Halberstam of the University of California, San Diego. According to Halberstam, in gothic novels and stories (a popular eighteenth- and nineteenth-century literary genre that emphasized the grotesque and mysterious) visual codes were routinely used to identify "good" from "bad" and socially acceptable from socially unacceptable. Thus, supposedly it was possible to tell if a person was "low-class," mentally inferior, or sexually perverse simply by observing their outward appearance. And the term "bad blood" became code for racial inferiority. The creature created by Victor Frankenstein, says Halberstam, walks, talks, and thinks. While secretly observing the De Lacey family, it educates itself and aspires to become truly human and take its place in society. But alas, it cannot overcome its physical "otherness," the visual deformity that in society's eyes proves its inferiority and monstrosity.

Beautiful!—Great God! His yellow skin scarcely covered the work of muscles and arteries beneath; his hair was of a lustrous black, and flowing; his teeth of a pearly whiteness; but these luxuriances only formed a more horrid contrast with his watery eyes, that seemed almost of the same colour as the dun white sockets in which they were set, his shrivelled complexion and straight black lips.

Excerpted from *Skin Shows: Gothic Horror and the Technology of Monsters*, by Judith Halberstam. Copyright 1995, Duke University Press. Reprinted by permission of the publisher.

Frankenstein's monster's skin barely covers his interior—the monster is transparent. The features that should make him beautiful, furthermore, "lustrous black" hair and "teeth of a pearly whiteness," look hideous because they are out of place in relation to the "watery eyes" and "shrivelled complexion." The monster is both skintight and "shrivelled," he has beautiful features set next to extreme ugliness. The whole impression is underscored by the "straight black lips"—evidence of a lack of internal circulation, evidence of the borrowed nature of all of his most necessary features. All in all, the monster is the obscenity of the surface, unwatchable, a masterpiece of a horror that cannot be viewed without terror.

It is no surprise that *Frankenstein* is the granddaddy of Gothic film horror. The horror film, after all, depends upon a certain degree of unwatchability. Cinematic horror also asks that the monster become a kind of screen onto which the spectator's fears are projected. In a way, *Frankenstein* establishes the preconditions for cinematic horror and for horror to become cinematic by making the monster's monstrosity so definitively visual. Only a blind man can accept the monster uncritically in this novel and, in a way, the blindness of old De Lacey represents also the blindness of the reader. We are disposed as readers to sympathize with the monster because, unlike the characters in the novel, we cannot see him. Once the monster becomes visible within contemporary horror films, monstrosity becomes less and less recuperable [recoverable].

VISUAL CODES AND RACE DISCRIMINATION

The monster in *Frankenstein* establishes visual horror as the main standard by which the monster judges and is judged. The most central episode in the novel, the narrative of the De Lacey family, establishes visual recognition as the most important code in the narrative of monstrosity. The story of the De Laceys is buried within the monster's story, their story is a subset of his, but his story (history) becomes a model of history itself as he learns of "the strange system of human society" and of "the division of property, of immense wealth and squalid poverty; of rank, descent, and noble blood."

Just as the monster reads *Paradise Lost* as "a true history," so "true history" is reduced to the story of one family at the innermost recess of the novel. True history and fiction trade places so that the story of the family replaces the story of na-

GOTHIC FICTION

Noted literary scholar and author Leonard Wolf here provides a useful definition of gothic literature and cites some well-known examples.

Gothic fiction, which emerged as a distinct kind of writing in the mid-eighteenth century, has, as its usual central figure, an indisputably virginal young woman of genteel breeding who finds herself set down in a tangle of misfortunes, the most frightful of which is that she is being pursued, through caverns or castle, through ruins or abbeys, by a looming, dark male figure who has something terribly threatening to women on his mind. B.G. MacCarthy, writing in *The Female Pen* (1947), describes the Gothic ambience as made up of "dizzying battlements, dark and winding stairways, dark dungeons, instruments of torture, groans and gouts of blood, secret passages with many a suggestion of spectral life, ghostly music, tapestries which sway with the wind and which betray the secret watcher or the assassin."

In Horace Walpole's *Castle of Otranto* (1764), the so-called first of the English Gothic fictions, the pursuit has hovering over it a delicate whiff of incest; while in Matthew Lewis's *The Monk* (1796), there is nothing delicate about the incest at all. There, Father Ambrosio, pure as the driven snow as the book begins, discovers debauchery [sexual excesses] and makes a career of it. As the tale ends, he learns that the woman he has murdered to get at her daughter is really his mother, and that the maiden he has ravished and killed is his sister. In Ann Radcliffe's considerably more refined *Mysteries of Udolpho* (1794), the terrors that engage a reader frequently appear to be supernatural, though they never are; while in Charles Maturin's *Melmoth the Wanderer* (1820), perhaps the greatest Gothic fiction yet written, the full complexity of the Faustian bargain [deal with the devil] is ironically explored.

Curiously enough, despite the achievements of such men as Walpole, Lewis, and Maturin, Gothic fiction, almost from its inception, had a special attraction for women. Indeed, in the early days of the genre, reading Gothic novels or writing them became a middle-class female preoccupation—as if women, oppressed by needlepoint, whalebone stays, psychological frustrations, shame, and babies, found in the reading or writing of these fictions a way to signal to each other, and perhaps to the world of men, the shadowy outlines of their own pain.

Leonard Wolf, ed., *The Annotated Frankenstein* (1818 text). New York: Clarkson S. Potter, 1977, pp. xii–xiv.

tions; and the narrative of the body replaces the history of creation; and the significance of visual codes becomes greater than that of heritage. The fiction of the monster replaces the history of discovery and invention that first Walton and then Frankenstein try to tell. And through these series of substitutions, the "true history" of the world boils down to the monster's reading list, a quirky canon of stories for underdogs, and a tale of subjectivity as a self-knowledge that inheres to the human.

But humanity as well as monstrosity, in this novel, depends upon visual codes for its construction. The women in Victor's family, Elizabeth, Caroline, and Justine, in their roles and fates in the novel, suggest the contradictions which lie at the heart of any attempt to distinguish definitively between human and monster. Elizabeth is rescued by Caroline from a peasant family. Caroline notices Elizabeth in the poor family's cottage because "she appeared of a different stock." Elizabeth is "thin and very fair" while the peasant children are "dark-eyed, hardy little vagrants." Indeed, it happens that Elizabeth is of "different stock" and the daughter of a nobleman, fit, therefore, for adoption. Caroline adopts Justine also but Justine must remain a servant since her heritage reveals no nobility. Birth, then, or blood rather, separates one woman from another and prepares one for marriage and the other for service. But notice that the difference between the noble and the debased is clearly exhibited in this instance upon the surface of the body—Elizabeth stands out from the rest of her poor family because she is thin and fair.

The class designation implied by "different stock," because it is a distinction based upon blood, exemplifies very well how . . . "racial discrimination" springs from the narrative. . . . Racial discrimination in *Frankenstein* [seems] to be a way of transforming class into a natural and immutable category, but as the difference in status between Elizabeth and Justine shows, the transformation is more complicated than this. By emphasizing that Elizabeth stands out from the "dark-eyed, hardy little vagrants" in the peasant family, Shelley betrays a class-biased belief that not only is nobility inherent but aristocratic class coincides with aristocratic race and is therefore *visible*. Race discrimination, indeed, displaces or at least supplements class hierarchies in this narrative partly because the theme of visible monstrosity demands that identity be something that can be seen. The monster, as we know, represents the threat not of a new class but of a new *race* of beings.

PERVERSE SEXUAL FEELINGS

The class gradations implied by the adoptions of Elizabeth as daughter and Justine as servant, then, hint at a tension within Shelley's writing between class, race, and gender. Both women are marked by their class (and class marking may be understood as race marking) in ways that make their Gothic fates inevitable. Elizabeth, as obviously middle class, must be sacrificed to the monster, and Justine, a lower-class servant, must stand in for the monster in the trial for the murder of William. On a certain level she doubles the female monster whose fate is always to be less than human. Configurations in the novel of class and gender, in fact, turn class into proletariat [laboring class], gender into woman and oppose the two in relation to the monster. In other words, the only category that remains unmarked in the novel, the only category that seems "natural" is that of the bourgeois [property-owning] male and he, in the form of Victor and Walton, consequently comes to embody the human.

Visual codes by the end of the century in Gothic fiction came to signify predispositions for crime or sexual aberration. As we . . . see in [Robert Louis] Stevenson's *Dr. Jekyll and Mr. Hyde* and [Bram] Stoker's *Dracula,* bad bodies are easily identifiable and demand expulsion. But criminal anthropology of the 1890s also made essential connections between outward appearance and inward essence and it is here that we can discuss a ripple of Gothic form across a variety of scientific, cultural, and social narratives. While visual horror in *Frankenstein* is the reason that the monster must live his days in exile, in fin-de-siècle [late-nineteenth-century] Gothic visual horror is the sign of a criminality that will demand expulsion. The difference between Frankensteinian horror and fin-de-siècle horror is . . . a result of different conceptions of subjectivity. Gothic narratives in fiction, science, and social science combined to produce evil or criminality as a seed planted deep within an interior self. But how did the self come to be associated with interiority and how did truth come to be represented by a deep structure of subjectivity? One answer surely lies in the eruption of "sexuality" in the nineteenth century, a discourse and a technology which . . . proliferates across disciplines. . . .

The Gothic monster is an excellent example of the secret of sexuality that is both hidden and revealed within the same text. But the monster is also an example of the way that sexuality is constructed *as* identity in a way that ignores all other identifying traits (race, class, and gender to name a few). In *Frankenstein* the monster is pre-sexual, his sexuality, in other words, does not constitute his identity. But that is not to say that sexual aberration is missing from Shelley's definition of monstrosity: simply, sexuality is always a part of other identifying traits. For example, the monster's status as sexual outlaw and social pariah [outcast] are mutually dependent. The endeavor of Frankenstein to first create life on his own and then to prevent his monster from mating suggests, if only by default, a homoerotic tension which underlies the incestuous bond. Frankenstein's voluntary exclusion from friends and family in pursuit of the secret of creating life also hints at the sexual nature of Victor's apparent withdrawal from all social intercourse. His creation of "a being like myself" hints at both masturbatory and homosexual desires which the scientist attempts to sanctify with the reproduction of another being. The suggestion that a homosexual bond in fact animates the plot adds an element of sexual perversity to the monster's already hybrid form. . . .

THE MONSTER MIXES HUMANITY WITH DEFORMITY

Sexual perversity and homosexual panic alone are not enough to characterize monstrosity. . . . Homophobia [hatred and fear of homosexuals] has a particular relation to the fear of femininity and that both play a part in class formations. Thus, the aristocracy, for example, a class in decline in the nineteenth century, may be feminized in relation to the "vigorous and productive values of the middle class" and certain behaviors previously associated with aristocrats . . . come to mark the homosexual. The sexually perverse can, in this way, be linked to a corrupt class (as it almost always was in early Gothic novels by Anne Radcliffe and Horace Walpole) and bad blood joins one to the other. But it is important to note the importance of race also within this topography of monstrosity; in the nineteenth century bad blood was becoming less and less a feature of old families and declining aristocrats and more an indicator of racial undesirability.

The connection between homosexuality and sociopolitical otherness can be made quite clear in terms of a belief in the inherent evil of certain groups of people. [Scholar] Hannah Arendt, in *The Origins of Totalitarianism*, makes the brilliant observation that crimes (the crime of being homosexual, the crime of being of the wrong race, i.e., Jewish) are turned into vices when a society is intent upon establishing a "world of fatalities." In such a world Jews, for example, and homosexuals are bound by birth to their anomalous status and, as Arendt writes: "The seeming broad-mindedness that equates crime and vice, if allowed to estabish its own code of law, will invariably prove more cruel and inhuman than laws, no matter how severe, which respect man's independent responsibility for his behavior." The opposition between crime and vice is extremely important to an examination of Gothic monstrosity. Frankenstein's monster argues that his "vices are the children of a forced solitude" but Victor thinks his monster, by virtue of his filthy form, was made to sin. Indeed, the equivocation between these two positions is unique to *Frankenstein* for, in the Gothic novel at the end of the nineteenth century, monsters are always born bad.

The homosexual subplot in *Frankenstein* props up an analogy between mixed blood and inherent perversity and suggests that while the "paranoid Gothic" is sustained on one level by a fear of sexuality between men, it also evinces a belief in the fixity of social relations and positions. Whatever disturbs these relations, this pattern, is "dirty" or "filthy" matter which must be excluded. But in *Frankenstein* the complexity of the monster—it walks, it talks, it demands, it pursues, it rationalizes and shows emotion—confuses the politics of purity in which every dirty thing is marked and will pollute if not eliminated. The monster mixes humanity with physical deformity, a desire for community with an irreducible foreignness, great physical strength with femininity.

We recall that Frankenstein agrees to make the monster a mate because he has been somewhat moved by his creation's eloquent pleas for tolerance. When the monster confronts his maker amid the sublime scenery of the Alps, he moves his author to feel compassion and "a wish to console him" but the sight of the monster still provokes horror: "when I saw the filthy mass that moved and talked, my heart sickened, and my feelings were altered to those of hatred and horror." This sequence plays out what is, in the context of the novel, a by now familiar opposition between language and vision in which the visual registers horror while language confers humanity. . . .

To Create a New Race?

But monstrosity is not simply a matter of appearance, and perhaps the opposition between language and vision is more entangled than the model of "imaginary" and "symbolic" may imply. It is precisely in the realm of the symbolic, in the realm of language, of course, that monstrosity and humanity emerge as inseparable. The episode in which Frankenstein talks himself out of creating a female monster, for example, is remarkable for the way that it reconstructs the monster's monstrosity not simply as a visual production but as the place where the not-human is inscribed. The monster represents the inscription of the not-human through monstrosity, he is its textual form, his autobiography is the history of Gothic, as we shall see.

Sitting in his laboratory one evening during his efforts to make his monster a mate, Frankenstein ponders what he is doing. He begins to reason with himself about the morality of his new labors and he considers, "she might become ten thousand times more malignant than her mate," and "she might turn in disgust from him to the superior beauty of man," finally, "one of the first sympathies for which the daemon thirsted would be children, and a race of devils would be propagated upon the earth." Here all compassion has been transformed into mistrustful fear. Frankenstein has not heard the monster's story at all and now he translates it into a demonic desire to populate the earth with a new race. . . . Was it not Frankenstein himself who had hoped that his scientific breakthrough would make him the creator of a new species? "A new species would bless me as its creator and source; many happy and excellent natures would owe their being to me. No father could claim the gratitude of his child so completely as I should deserve theirs.". . .

Every time Frankenstein constructs his creation as monstrous, he renders invisible, immutable, and ineffable his own humanity. The self-evident nature of the "human" is constructed in Gothic as the destruction or inscription of the other. Visibility, I have been arguing, is the index of monstrosity in *Frankenstein* even as invisibility and ineffability imply humanity. Because of its readability, monstrosity allows us a peek at the construction of otherness out of the raw materials of racial undesirability, class definition, family ties, sexual perversity, and gender instability. The monster, therefore, by embodying what is not human, produces the human as a discursive effect. The human in *Frankenstein*, of course, is the Western European, bourgeois, male scientist. But monstrosity, I suggested early on, is inextricably bound to textuality, to the novelistic in particular, and so it is not surprising to discover that the history of Gothic monstrosity or embodied fear overlaps significantly with the history of the novel.

Abandonment and Lack of Proper Nurture Shape the Monster's Nature

Anne K. Mellor

In this informative essay, Anne K. Mellor, a professor of English at UCLA and noted biographer of Mary Shelley, examines some of the Monster's most basic feelings, including rejection, loneliness, and revenge. These emotions, Mellor suggests, mirror those of Mary Shelley herself, who to a marked degree felt abandoned when, long after her mother's death, her father, William Godwin, took a second wife. As Mellor explains, Mary Shelley's ideas about proper nurturing and education, which she deemed essential to growing into a healthy, virtuous adult, were shaped by the writings of seventeenth-century French philosopher Jean Jacques Rousseau, seventeenth-century English philosopher John Locke, and eighteenth-century English physician and philosopher David Hartley. Mellor also mentions "The Rime of the Ancient Mariner," by English poet Samuel Taylor Coleridge (1772–1834), as influencing the portrayal of the Monster's abandonment and loneliness.

As she wrote out her novel, Mary Shelley distanced herself from her originating dream-identification with the anxious and rejecting parent and focused instead on the plight of the abandoned child. Increasingly she identified with the orphaned creature. The heart of this three-volume novel is the creature's account of his own development, which occupies all but thirty pages of the second volume of the first edition. And in this volume, Mary Shelley spoke most directly in her own voice: Percy Shelley's manuscript revisions are far less numerous in Volume

II than in Volumes I or III. As she described the creature's first experiences in the world and his desperate attempts to establish a bond of affection with the De Lacey family, Mary Shelley was clearly drawing on her own experiences of emotional isolation in the Godwin household. Specific links join the creature's life to Mary Shelley's own. The creature reads about his conception in the journal of lab reports he grabbed up as he fled from Victor Frankenstein's laboratory; Mary Shelley could have read about her own conception in Godwin's Diary (where he noted the nights on which he and Mary Wollstonecraft had sexual intercourse during their courtship with a "Chez moi" or a "Chez elle", including every night but two between December 20, 1796, and January 3, 1797). Both the creature and Mary Shelley read the same books. In the years before and during the composition of *Frankenstein*, Mary Shelley read or reread the books found by the creature in an abandoned portmanteau—Goethe's *Werther*, Plutarch's *Lives of the Noble Romans*, Volney's *Ruins or, . . . the Revolutions of Empire*, and Milton's *Paradise Lost*, as well as the poets the creature occasionally quotes, Coleridge and Byron. Moreover, as a motherless child and a woman in a patriarchal culture, Mary Shelley shared the creature's powerful sense of being born without an identity, without role-models to emulate, without a history. The creature utters a *cri de coeur* [cry from the heart] that was Mary Shelley's own: "Who was I? What was I? Whence did I come? What was my destination? These questions continually recurred, but I was unable to solve them."

LIKE A WILD BEAST

What the creature does know is that a child deprived of a loving family becomes a monster. Again and again he insists that he was born good but compelled by others into evil: "I was benevolent and good; misery made me a fiend." Granted a mate, he will become good again: "My vices are the children of a forced solitude that I abhor; and my virtues will necessarily arise when I live in communion with an equal." Even after the destruction of all his hopes has condemned him to unremitting vengeance, the creature still insists, "I had feelings of affection, they were requited by detestation and scorn."

The creature's argument is derived in part from Rousseau's *Emile*, which Mary Shelley read in 1816. Rousseau claimed that "God makes all things good; man meddles with them and they become evil." He blamed the moral failings of children specifically upon the absence of a mother's love. Attacking mothers who refuse to nurse or care for their own children in early infancy, Rousseau insists, in a comment that self-servingly ignores a father's parental responsibilities (Rousseau abandoned his own children at the local orphanage):

> Would you restore all men to their primal duties, begin with the mothers; the results will surprise you. Every evil follows in the train of this first sin; the whole moral order is disturbed, nature is quenched in every breast, the home becomes gloomy, the spectacle of a young family no longer stirs the husband's love and the stranger's reverence.

Without mothering, without an early experience of a loving education, writes Rousseau in a statement that the creature's experience vividly confirms, "a man left to himself from

LOCKE ON A HEALTHY EDUCATION

The late James G. Clapp, a noted authority on John Locke, here summarizes the philosopher's emphasis on attention, love, and proper nurturing for the development of a well-educated and self-actualized individual. Tellingly, these are the very emotional elements missing from the Monster's life in Mary Shelley's novel.

In 1693 Locke . . . published the contents as *Some Thoughts Concerning Education* in response to "so many, who profess themselves at a loss how to breed their children." His thought was marked by a ready understanding of, and warm sympathy with, children. Three main thoughts dominate the work. First, the individual aptitudes, capacities, and idiosyncrasies [personal traits] of the child should govern learning, not arbitrary curricular or rote learning taught by the rod. Second, Locke placed the health of the body and the development of a sound character ahead of intellectual learning. In the third place, he saw that play, high spirits, and the "gamesome humor" natural to children should govern the business of learning wherever possible. Compulsory learning is irksome; where there is play in learning, there will be joy in it. Throughout he placed emphasis on good example, practice, and use rather than on precepts, rules, and punishment. The work was an implicit criticism of his own education at Westminster and Oxford, which he found unpleasant and largely useless.

Writing almost as a physician, Locke advised "plenty of open air, exercise, and sleep; plain diet, no wine or strong drink, and very little or no physic [medicine or drugs]; not too warm and strait [tight-fitting] clothing; especially the head and feet kept birth would be more of a monster than the rest."

Mary Shelley powerfully evoked the creature's psychic response to the conviction that he is destined to be forever an outcast, as alone as the Ancient Mariner on his wide, wide sea—a horrifying spectacle that had haunted Mary Shelley's imagination since she heard Coleridge recite the poem in 1806. Again and again the creature cries out:

> Every where I see bliss, from which I alone am irrevocably excluded.
>
> I had never yet seen a being resembling me, or who claimed any intercourse with me. What was I?
>
> Increase of knowledge only discovered to me more clearly what a wretched outcast I was. . . . no Eve soothed my sorrows, or shared my thoughts; I was alone.

---

cold, and the feet often used to cold water and exposed to wet." The aim in all was to keep the body in strength and vigor, able to endure hardships.

Locke urged that early training must establish the authority of the parents so that good habits may be established. The prime purpose is the development of virtue, the principle of which is the power of denying ourselves the satisfaction of our desires. The child should be taught to submit to reason when young. Parents teach by their own example. They should avoid severe punishments and beatings as well as artificial rewards. Rules should be few when a child is young, but those few should be obeyed. Mild, firm, and rational approval or disapproval are most effective in curbing bad behavior. Children should be frequently in the company of their parents, who should in turn study the disposition of the child and endeavor to use the child's natural desire for freedom and play to make learning as much like recreation as possible. High spirits should not be curbed, but turned to creative use. Curiosity too should be encouraged, and questions should be heard and fairly answered. Cruelty must always be discouraged and courageousness approved.

As the child grows, familiarity should be increased so that the parent has a friend in the mature child. Virtue, breeding. and a free liberal spirit as well as wisdom and truthfulness were the goals set by Locke in all his advice. Affection and friendship were for him both means and ends of good education.

Paul Edwards, ed., *The Encyclopedia of Philosophy.* New York: Macmillan, 1967, vol. 4, pp. 500–501.

Here Mary Shelley unearthed her own buried feelings of parental abandonment and forced exile from her father. Her creature, disappointed in his long-cherished desire for a welcome from the De Lacey family, feels anger, then a desire for revenge, and finally a violent severing from all that is human, civilized, cultural. "I was like a wild beast that had broken the toils; destroying the objects that obstructed me, and ranging through the wood with a stag-like swiftness. . . . All, save I, were at rest or in enjoyment: I, like the arch-fiend, bore a hell within me." . . . The image of a beast breaking out of harness focuses her argument that a human being deprived of companionship, of nurturing, of mothering, is driven beyond the pale of humanity. The creature has crossed the barrier that separates the human from the bestial, the domesticated from the wild, the cooked from the raw. Symbolically, the creature turns his acculturated love-gifts of firewood back into raw fire by burning the De Lacey cottage to the ground while dancing round it, himself consumed in a frenzy of pure hatred and revenge.

INFANTICIDE

Searching for his only legitimate parent, the creature encounters outside Geneva the five-year-old William Frankenstein. Once more thwarted in his desire for a family when the child refuses to accompany him, his anger claims—perhaps unintentionally—its first human sacrifice. Here . . . Mary Shelley is uncovering her own repressed aggression. For it can be no accident that the creature's first victim is the exact image of her son William, named after his grandfather Godwin. Having felt rejected by her father, emotionally when he married Mary Jane Clairmont and overtly when she eloped with Percy Shelley, Mary had long repressed a hostility to Godwin that erupted in the murder of his namesake. It is actually his double namesake, since Godwin had given the name William to his own son, who was the favored child in the Godwin-Clairmont household, tenderly nicknamed Love-will by his doting mother. This murder thus raises to consciousness one of the most deeply buried fears energizing Mary Shelley's original dream: *might I be capable of murdering my own flesh and blood?* For William Frankenstein is a deliberate portrait of William Shelley: he has the same "lively blue eyes, dimpled cheeks, and endearing manners," the same "dark eyelashes and curling hair" and propensity to take little *wives,* Louisa Biron being William Frankenstein's favorite playmate, where Allegra Byron was William Shelley's choice. The creature's calculated strangling of the blue-eyed, blond-haired, manly boy articulates both Mary Shelley's horrified recognition that she is capable of imagining the murder of her own child—capable of infanticide itself—and her instinctive revulsion against that act. As she suggests, a rejected and unmothered child can become a killer, especially the killer of its own parents, siblings, children. When the nuclear family fails to mother its offspring, it engenders homicidal monsters.

THE MONSTER'S MIND A BLANK SLATE?

And yet, even without mothering, the creature manages to gain an education. Mary Shelley's allusion to Rousseau's theory of the natural man as a noble savage, born free but everywhere in chains and inevitably corrupted by society, focuses one of the minor concerns of the novel, its theory of education. In the great debate on the relative importance of nature versus nurture, on whether learning achievements should be attributed primarily to innate intelligence or to social environments, Mary Shelley was convinced that nurture is crucial. Her reading of Rousseau's *Second Discourse* had given her insight into the limitations of the natural man as well as the potential evils of civilization. Her creature *is* Rousseau's natural man, a creature no different from the animals, responding unconsciously to the needs of his flesh and the changing conditions of his environment. He feels pleasure at the sight of the moon, the warmth of the sun, the sounds of bird-song, the light and heat of fire; pain at the coldness of snow, the burning sensation of fire, the pangs of hunger and thirst. In the state of nature, man is free and unselfconscious; insofar as he can gratify his primal desires easily, he is happy. For Frankenstein's creature, a dry hovel is "paradise, compared to the bleak forest, my former residence, the rain-dropping branches, and dank earth." But as Rousseau also emphasized, especially in *The Social Contract,* the natural man lacks much: language, the capacity to think rationally, companionship and the affections that flow from it, a moral consciousness. Peering through the chinks of his hovel, Mary Shelley's creature rapidly discovers the limitations of the state of nature and the positive benefits of a civilization grounded on family life.

Even though she depicts Frankenstein's creature as Rousseau's natural man, even though she echoes Rousseau's *Emile* at critical points, she does not endorse Rousseau's view that the simple gratification of human passions will lead to virtuous behavior. Her account of the creature's mental and moral development is more closely allied to the . . . theories of David Hartley and John Locke. The associationist David Hartley argued that early sensative experiences determine adult behavior, and the rationalist John Locke concurred that natural man is neither innately good nor innately evil, but rather a white paper or blank slate upon which sensations write impressions that then become ideas or conscious experience. The creature's moral development closely parallels the paradigm that Hartley laid out in his *Observations of Man, His Frame, His Duty, and His Expectations* (1749) and follows the theories that Locke propounded first in 1690 in his *Essay Concerning Human Understanding* (which Mary Shelley read in 1816) and later in the more pragmatically oriented *Some Thoughts Concerning Education* (1693). The creature first experiences purely physical and undifferentiated sensations of light, darkness, heat, cold, hunger, pain and pleasure; this is the earliest period of infancy when "no distinct ideas occupied my mind; all was confused." Gradually, the creature learns to distinguish his sensations and thus his "mind received every day additional ideas." At the same time he learns the causes of his feelings of pain or pleasure, and how to produce the effects he desires by obtaining clothing, shelter, food and fire.

THE MONSTER EDUCATES HIMSELF

The creature's education is completed in just the way Locke advocates, by providing him with examples of moral and intellectual virtue. As Locke insisted:

> Of all the ways whereby children are to be instructed, and their manners formed, the plainest, easiest, and most efficacious, is to set before their eyes the examples of those things that you would have them do or avoid. . . . Virtues and vices can by no words be so plainly set before their understandings as the actions of other men will show them.

When the creature stares through the chink in the wall of his hovel into the adjoining cottage, he sees before him a living illustration of benevolence, affection, industry, thrift, and natural justice in the actions of the De Lacey family. The De

Laceys embody Mary Shelley's ideal of the egalitarian family—with one important exception: they lack a mother. The De Laceys not only stimulate the creature's emotions and arouse his desire to do good to others (which takes the form of gathering firewood for them), but also introduce him to the concept and function of a spoken and written language. Here adopting a referential theory of language, in which sounds or words are conceived as pointing to objects or mental states, Mary Shelley traces the creature's linguistic development from his earliest acquisition of nouns and proper names through his grasp of abstractions to his ability to speak, read, and finally write, the latter processes enabled by his overhearing Safie's French lessons in the next room and by his acquisition of a private library. While Locke's insistence that children learn best from examples now seems commonplace, . . . Locke was the first educator to recognize that human rationality and the capacity for self-discipline evolve gradually in the growing child and that the subject-matter to be learned must be adapted to the differential capacities of children at different stages of development.

The creature learns from sensations and examples; what he learns is determined by his environment. The De Lacey family provides a lesson in almost perfect virtue, grounded in the private domestic affections, together with a treatise on social and human injustice as practiced in the public realm by the law courts of France and Safie's ungrateful Turkish father. The creature's knowledge of human vice and virtue is further enlarged by his reading. From Plutarch's *Lives of the Noble Romans* he learns the nature of heroism and public virtue and civic justice; from Volney's *Ruins, or A Survey of the Revolutions of Empires* he learns the contrasting nature of political corruption and the causes of the decline of civilizations; from Milton's *Paradise Lost* he learns the origins of human good and evil and the roles of the sexes; and from Goethe's *Werther* he learns the range of human emotions, from domestic love to suicidal despair, as well as the rhetoric in which to articulate not only ideas but feelings.

VICTOR FRANKENSTEIN'S EDUCATION

The creature's excellent education, which includes moral lessons garnered from the two books Locke thought essential, Aesop's Fables and the Bible, is implicitly contrasted to the faulty education received by Victor Frankenstein. While

Alphonse Frankenstein initially followed Godwin's pedagogical precepts [ideas about educating children]—he inspired his children to learn in a noncompetitive atmosphere by encouraging their voluntary desire to please others and by giving them practical goals (one learns a foreign language in order to read the interesting books in that tongue)—he failed to monitor sufficiently closely the books that Victor Frankenstein actually read. Instead of the Bible, Aesop, and *Robinson Crusoe* recommended by Godwin, Locke, and Rousseau, Victor devoured the misleading alchemical treatises of [medieval researchers and delvers into magic] Cornelius Agrippa, Paracelsus, and Albertus Magnus, books which encouraged, not an awareness of human folly and injustice, but rather a hubristic [arrogant] desire for human omnipotence, for the gaining of the philosopher's stone and the elixir of life.

Mary Shelley's pedagogy, derived in large part from her father's espousal of Locke, emphasizes the role of the affections in the education of young children. Victor learns because he wishes to please his father, Elizabeth because she wishes to delight her aunt, the creature because he wishes to emulate and be accepted by the De Lacey family. Clearly an unloved child will not learn well—the creature's education is effectively ended when the De Laceys abandon him. But how well does even a much-loved child learn? Victor Frankenstein was such, but his father's indulgence only encouraged his son's egotistical dreams of omnipotence. In this Mary Shelley reveals her nagging doubt whether even a supportive family can produce a virtuous adult. In the successes and failures of both the creature's and Frankenstein's education, Mary Shelley registered a pervasive maternal anxiety: *even if I love and nurture my child, even if I provide the best education of which I am capable, I may still produce a monster—and who is responsible for that*?

NO ESCAPE EXCEPT IN DEATH

Behind Mary Shelley's maternal anxieties lies a more general problem, the problem posed for her by Rousseau's writings. For Rousseau had made it clear that the movement away from the state of nature into the condition of civilization entails a loss of freedom, a frustration of desire, and an enclosure within the prisonhouse of language or . . . the symbolic order. Civilization produces as much discontent as content. In place of the natural man's instinctive harmony with his surroundings, society substitutes a system of conflicting economic interests and a struggle for individual mastery, an aggressive competition restrained by but not eliminated from Rousseau's favored constitutional democracy. For once the creature has left the state of nature and learned the language and laws of society, he has gained a self-consciousness that he can never lose, the consciousness of his own isolation:

> I learned that the possessions most esteemed by your fellow-creatures were, high and unsullied [pure] descent united with riches . . . but . . . I possessed no money, no friends, no kind of property. I was, besides, endowed with a figure hideously deformed and loathsome; . . . When I looked around, I saw and heard of none like me. . . .

> I cannot describe to you the agony that these reflections inflicted upon me; I tried to dispel them, but sorrow only increased with knowledge. Oh, that I had for ever remained in my native wood, nor known or felt beyond the sensations of hunger, thirst, and heat!

Deprived of all human companionship, the creature can never recover from the disease of self-consciousness; for him, no escape, save death, is possible. In this context, the novel points up the irony implicit in Locke's most famous pedagogical maxim: "A sound mind in a sound body is a short but full description of a happy state in this world." Exercise and good diet can produce the healthy body Locke found so conducive to the development of mental and moral capacities; but can the creature, born with a grotesquely oversized and unsound body, ever develop a sound mind? Or, in the terms posed for Shelley by David Hartley, can an unmothered child whose formative experiences are of pain rather than pleasure ever develop a rational intellect, a healthy moral sense, or a normal personality?

Victor and His Creation Struggle with Gender Identity

William Patrick Day

This intriguing psychological analysis of Mary Shelley's *Frankenstein* is by William Patrick Day, who teaches English at Oberlin College in Ohio. One key to understanding the novel, Day suggests, is the emotional (and sometimes physical) state known as androgyny, the possession of a combination of both male and female characteristics (and usually the inability to achieve a firm identity in either role). Victor Frankenstein desires to fulfill the masculine role society expects of him, but he repeatedly fails to play that role effectively. Conversely, his creation, the Monster, longs to enter the female-dominated world of the loving family, but he too cannot achieve his goal. As the monster becomes stronger and therefore more "masculine," Day contends, Victor becomes increasingly passive and therefore more "feminine." By creating his "son" the Monster, for instance, and thereby completing the act of reproduction without the need of a woman, Victor in a sense assumes a woman's traditional role. It should be emphasized that Day does not suggest that Mary Shelley consciously incorporated these ideas when writing the book; rather, as does all great literature, in exploring the complexities of human life the work captures, even if inadvertently, many of the subtleties of human emotions and relationships; these subtleties become fair game for scholars to discover and analyze.

Frankenstein is subtitled *The New Prometheus*, but it might easily be called *Men without Women*. Mary Shelley develops and refines the themes that her father [William Godwin] laid out in [his novel] *Caleb Williams.* Victor Frankenstein's assertion of his masculine identity and rejection of his feminine, affectional family becomes a confrontation with his own doubled nature and potential androgyny.... He tries to create his own identity outside legitimate channels, though rather than attempting to become his own son, Victor builds his offspring in the laboratory. The line of inheritance in *Frankenstein* is ... weak and corrupt ... for Victor refuses to take the responsibility for his creation.... Victor cannot sustain his masculine identity and power, and his creature wrecks [destruction] upon his family. ... In doing so, the creature performs the violent acts that Victor wants but cannot acknowledge to himself. The restless desire to be rid of suffocating powerlessness, leads the masculine self, once "free" of the affectional and feminine, to confrontation with that side of its nature and, inevitably, to self-destruction.

ATTRACTIVE ALTERNATIVES TO ARCTIC HORROR

The conflict between the masculine and the feminine is embodied in the opposition between male isolation and the feminine family. The three concentric rings of the novel all repeat this dynamic: Walton's rejection of his sister, Mrs. Saville and her family in England; Victor's rejection of his family, shortly after his mother's death, for six years at the university; and finally, the creature's rejection by the Delacy family. The dynamic is not, of course, quite the same in all instances: Walton and Victor have parallel experiences, while the creature reverses their pattern. Walton and Victor both leave behind the world of women in favor of those of men—the sea or the university—but the creature desperately wants to enter the world of women and the family. Strikingly, when he cannot do this, he forms a male community of two, himself and Victor, though Victor is an unwilling partner in this enterprise. The stories of all three men end in the icy polar wastes, identified as the scene of purely masculine activity—the search for power and fame—and finally the world of death.

The families in the novel all appear, at least at first, as attractive alternatives to arctic horror. The Frankensteins are close and loving, though this love is mainly showered on young Victor, who conceives of himself as the center of his family's life. Even more the quintessential feminine family are the Delacys, whom the creature watches through a chink in the wall. In his view, the Delacys are wonderfully happy, spending their whole lives loving and caring for one another. The family appears to be a safe haven, a refuge from the outside world. But these two families are literally refugees. The Delacys are outcasts, accepted neither by Christians nor Muslims, and the Frankensteins are a collection of strays. Caroline, Elizabeth, and Justine, who, though a servant, is like a member of the family, come from families that have broken up, primarily for economic reasons. The make-up of these families signals their essential weakness and the precarious place of the affectional ideal in the world. The creature yearns for a family only because he has never had one; based on their experiences, Victor and Walton both flee their families, though at the same time, each longs for that haven they have deprived themselves of, Walton by leaving it, and Victor by allowing the creature to destroy it.

ESCAPING THE THREAT OF INCEST

The failure of the affectional family here lies in more than its weakness in relation to the external world. Its structure is fundamentally incestuous. Caroline, Victor's mother, is the Baron Frankenstein's former ward, and Elizabeth, Victor's intended bride, has been raised as his sister. Walton's family is really just his sister, and his attachment to her carries with it the hint of incest. The creature's plan for starting a family in the Andes also falls into this pattern; since Victor will have to build his mate, she will in effect be his sister. Thus, Victor allows his family to be murdered by the creature because in doing so the creature wipes out the image of an incestuous, powerless identity from which Victor desperately wishes to escape. Though Victor over and over professes his love for his family and for his friend Clerval, he does nothing to protect them; only after they are gone does he actively pursue the creature. Indeed, through what we can only see as an unconscious self-delusion, he refuses to recognize that the creature's threat, "I will be with you on your wedding night," is directed, not at him, but at Elizabeth. Victor should realize this, since the threat is made just after Victor has destroyed the creature's mate, but instead he allows the creature to take his place in the marriage bed with Elizabeth and murder her. This destroys Victor's family, but it also removes the suffocating threat of incest and ends forever the fear of being drawn back into that world where masculine identity is submerged in the affective chaos in which distinctions between mother, sister, daughter, husband, brother, and son are erased.

TWO SIDES TO THEIR NATURES

Victor builds his creature as an act of self-assertion, of identity making. By creating life in his laboratory, he achieves the power of God, and indeed, he states that he hopes his creature will worship him. He has also usurped the power of the feminine, for he has reproduced without a woman. He thus seizes power that should not be his and establishes his own patriarchal line. He at first seems a sharp contrast to the figures of male authority that appear in the novel; Delacy is blind and enfeebled, Baron Frankenstein is ineffectual and hardly present, and the two scientists Victor works with at the university are men of learning without power. But his power is soon undermined by what he has wrought. The creature he has built is Victor's family. Clearly his son, the creature is also his brother and his double, for what Victor makes, he is. As the creature comes to dominate Victor, taunting him with his superior strength, depriving him of his sister-bride on his wedding night, he becomes Victor's father figure. The night he brings the creature to life, Victor dreams first of Elizabeth, then of his dead mother in her shroud; he awakens to see the creature standing by him. The creature is in this way also identified with Victor's mother and sister-fiancée. All of Victor's family relationships—with Caroline, the baron, Elizabeth, with Clerval, his virtual brother—are contained in his relationship to his creature, who is not simply the projection of Victor's masculine identity but also of his feminine side. The relationship that Victor thought would magnify his masculine identity in fact renders it intensely unstable by forcing upon him its contradictions and tensions.

The creature, huge, powerful, ugly, is . . . a parody of Victor's dream of masculine power. Victor flees the creature because the externalized image of the masculine archetype terrifies him; he does not want to acknowledge that this is the image of what he aspires to. Insofar as the creature is the projection of Victor's masculine archetype and aspiration, his destruction of the Frankensteins reflects Victor's own desires and impulses. But the creature is not simply raw, untamed, masculine power; Victor in fact forces him to become this in order to avoid accepting his own responsibility. The creature has two sides to his nature: physically he is grotesquely masculine, but his sensibility is essentially feminine. He loves music, is easily moved by the scenes in the Delacy house, and wants nothing more than to be part of an affective circle of relationships. Rejected by both Victor and the Delacys because of his horrifying appearance, his feminine half withers, starved for affection. As the creature gradually becomes more and more masculine, Victor becomes more and more passive; whenever the creature does something terrible, Victor collapses into illness and delirium. He both avoids responsibility for the creature's acts, and shows himself to be the submissive partner of the pair.

DEATH THE ONLY ESCAPE

Victor's responses are founded in his refusal to accept the fact of the creature's androgynous nature. Were he to accept the creature's capacity for affect, his feminine side, Victor would not only have to accept responsibility for his violence, the result of ill treatment, but he would also have to accept that his own masculine identity coexists with a feminine one, because the creature is Victor's double. Victor will play the passive role while the creature acts out the unconscious violence in Victor's attitude toward his family, but once that violence is complete, Victor attempts to seize again the masculine role and destroy what he has created. What Victor fights is, not simply a double who threatens his identity, but a double who reveals far too much about his own identity to him. The creature shows Victor the truth about his own nature; in seeking to destroy him, Victor is trying to destroy that truth, just as he allowed the creature to destroy the family that represented the externalization of his feminine half.

The creature, a completely unique being, becomes the nexus in which all of Victor's struggles with his own identity are made clear. The creature's androgyny challenges Victor, and he fails the first test: he can build the creature, but he cannot accept his connection to him. The creature's demands that Victor accept their relationship terrify him because they call upon the feminine, affective side of his nature, which he wants to escape. Victor's only response is to establish the pattern of sadomasochistic violence, first between the creature and the Frankensteins, then between the creature and himself. In order to preserve the illusion of his own exclusively masculine identity, Victor will die, for death is the only escape from the androgyny implied in the act of creation and the creature himself. Once he has forced the creature into conforming to the masculine archetype, Victor cannot then subdue and dominate him. He would rather they both die than put aside the masculine and come to the reconciliation that would synthesize the masculine and feminine halves in each.

Tampering in God's Domain

Timothy J. Madigan

Though written almost two centuries ago, Mary Shelley's *Frankenstein* is today more relevant than ever because scientists, through discoveries in genetics, the achievement of cloning, and the creation of artificial intelligence (computers), have lately begun to break through the barrier separating human knowledge from the secrets of life. In this thoughtful essay, scholar Timothy J. Madigan calls the fascination for and drive to find these secrets the "Frankenstein Impulse." Characters in hundreds of books, stories, and movies about such cutting-edge scientists, often of the "mad" variety, have frequently called it "tampering in God's domain," or words to that effect. Madigan here suggests that it is useless, and indeed impossible, to eradicate the Frankenstein Impulse. It is better for those who worry about the possible disastrous consequences of such research, he says, to expend their energy attempting to channel the impulse in constructive directions.

"You seek for knowledge and wisdom, as I once did; and I ardently hope that the gratification of your wishes may not be a serpent to sting you, as mine has been . . . I imagine that you may deduce an apt moral from my tale, one that may direct you if you succeed in your undertaking and console you in case of failure."

—Victor Frankenstein

The April 1994 issue of the Christian journal *First Things* has an interesting article by David R. Carlin, a former member of the Rhode Island Senate, entitled "For Luddite Humanism." In it, he bemoans the recent attempt by two researchers at George Washington University Medical Center to clone human embryos. Such a procedure, he argues, is

Reprinted from Timothy J. Madigan, "Defending Dr. Frankenstein," *Free Inquiry*, vol. 14, no. 4, pp. 48–50, by permission. (Endnotes in the original have been omitted in this reprint.)

dehumanizing, and he calls for a moral Ludditism—a rejection of technological tampering with humanness. "Unless that cultural revolution I mentioned earlier comes along [Carlin states], displacing America's regnant secularism [nonreligious outlook], the world will become increasingly safe not only for abortion but for euthanasia [mercy killing], cloning, and numerous other anti-human perversities."

Carlin is criticizing what might be called the "Frankenstein Impulse"—the desire to alter human nature, even to the point of creating life itself. Frankenstein is usually accused of having the character defect of hubris [extreme arrogance], attempting to be like God. And, like other mythical characters, such as Oepidus, it is hubris that causes his downfall. However, we would do well to reexamine Mary Shelley's classic 1818 novel in light of present-day advances and see what lesson it really holds for us.

COWARDICE RATHER THAN ARROGANCE

Was Mary Shelley denouncing hubris? It is important to keep in mind that the nineteen-year-old author was raised in a freethought household. Her parents and their friends were very much Enlightenment rationalists. Her father, William Godwin, was a noted Utilitarian philosopher and social critic, infamous in his day for his excoriations [denunciations] of churches and clerics, and her mother (who died when she was but a few days old) was Mary Wollstonecraft, author of the early feminist tract *A Vindication of the Rights of Woman.* In addition, her lover during the time of writing *Frankenstein* (and her future husband) was the poet Percy Shelley, who was expelled from Oxford for co-authoring the pamphlet *The Necessity of Atheism.* Mary Shelley, then, was not reared in a pious religious tradition and had no qualms about humans playing God, since for her the role remained unfilled by any deity.

It is also known that she took a keen interest in the scientific investigations of her day, especially those that dealt with the origins of life. Peter Haining, editor of *The Frankenstein Omnibus,* speaks about one of early nineteenth-century England's scientific experimenters, Andrew Crosse, who attempted to vivify inanimate objects using electricity. "Crosse was, though—like Frankenstein—a much misunderstood man, and found it difficult to get people to give a fair hearing to his beliefs about the boundless potential of electricity. However, at one of his lectures in London, on December 28, 1814, among his audience were

VICTOR FRANKENSTEIN'S INSPIRATION

This is the scene in the novel in which Victor attends a lecture by the highly respected Professor Waldman, whose remarks about science's untapped potential for good inspire the younger man to discover the fundamental secrets of nature.

He began his lecture by recapitulation of the history of chemistry and the various improvements made by different men of learning, pronouncing with fervour the names of the most distinguished discoverers. He then took a cursory [hasty] view of the present state of the science and explained many of its elementary terms. After having made a few preparatory experiments, he concluded with a panegyric [speech or hymn of praise] upon modern chemistry, the terms of which I shall never forget:—

'The ancient teachers of this science,' said he, 'promised impossibilities and performed nothing. The modern masters promise very little; they know that metals cannot be transmuted and that the elixir of life is a chimera [imaginary mythical creature]. But these philosophers, whose hands seem only made to dabble in dirt, and their eyes to pore over the microscope or crucible, have indeed performed miracles. They penetrate into the recesses of nature and show how she works in her hiding-places. They ascend into the heavens; they have discovered how the blood circulates, and the nature of the air we breathe. They have acquired new and almost unlimited powers; they can command the thunders of heaven, mimic the earthquake, and even mock the invisible world with its own shadows.'

Such were the professor's words—rather let me say such the words of the fate—enounced to destroy me. As he went on I felt as if my soul were grappling with a palpable enemy; one by one the various keys were touched which formed the mechanism of my being; chord after chord was sounded, and soon my mind was filled with one thought, one conception, one purpose. So much has been done, exclaimed the soul of Frankenstein—more, far more, will I achieve; treading in the steps already marked, I will pioneer a new way, explore unknown powers, and unfold to the world the deepest mysteries of creation.

Mary Shelley, *Frankenstein or the Modern Prometheus.* Ed. Maurice Hindle. New York: Penguin Books, 1985, pp. 95–96.

Percy and Mary Shelley—a fact Mary recorded in her diaries." This was three years before the publication of her novel.

The several film adaptations of this work have given it a "spooky" and horrific quality that is not found in the book itself. In fact, *Frankenstein* is better described as one of the earliest works of science fiction, rather than a work of horror. It has no supernatural quality. Victor Frankenstein does not live in a castle in Transylvania, aided by a hunchback assistant. Instead, he is a medical student (not even a doctor!) in Germany, and he performs his famed creation in what is essentially his dorm room. A brilliant researcher, Victor is plagued by questions. "Whence, I often asked myself, did the principle of life proceed? It was a bold question, and one which has ever been considered as a mystery; yet with how many things are we upon the brink of becoming acquainted, if cowardice or carelessness did not restrain our inquiries." These were the very types of questions that fascinated Mary and Percy Shelley.

If Frankenstein can be faulted—as indeed he can—it is not for hubris, but rather for the very qualities he mentions above, cowardice and carelessness. For he performs his operation without telling anyone else and, when his creation comes to life, he rejects it by running away and hoping the creature will die. This rejection of what he has brought about and his failure to share his findings with the scientific community or the people around him ultimately leads to tragedy, for the misbegotten creature—unloved and ill-treated—gets his revenge by killing all of Victor's loved ones, who remained in the dark about his very existence.

A POSITIVE EVALUATION OF HUMAN NATURE

It is significant that Mary Shelley subtitled her novel "The Modern Prometheus." Like her husband, she was fascinated by this ancient myth. While she was completing her novel, Percy Shelley was hard at work on his own masterpiece, the epic poem *Prometheus Unbound*. In it, the Titan realizes that what has kept him chained to the rocks for centuries was not the power of Zeus, but rather the hatred in his own heart. Once he retracts the curse he has placed on Zeus, murmuring "I wish no living thing to suffer pain," the chains fall from him, and Zeus topples from his throne. The peoples of the world, inspired by Prometheus' compassion, unite as one, forgetting their own age-old hatreds and finally using the gifts of technology he had bestowed upon them for peaceful ends. Who can forget the closing stanza:

To suffer woes which Hope thinks infinite;
To forgive wrongs darker than death or night;
To defy Power, which seems omnipotent;

To love, and bear; to hope till Hope creates
From its own wreck the thing it contemplates;
Neither to change, nor falter, nor repent;
This, like thy glory, Titan, is to be
Good, great and joyous, beautiful and free;
This is alone Life, Joy, Empire, and Victory.

Prometheus Unbound, an optimistic hymn to the potential-ities of human beings working together to solve their com-mon problems and a celebration of intellectual audacity, was published in 1820. Yet one senses that Mary Shelley did not completely share her husband's positive evaluation of human nature. She was rather more cautionary. Her Promethean fig-ure, Victor Frankenstein, does not live up to his role model. He lacks compassion for his creation (perhaps a reflection on the lack of belief in a benevolent deity in which Mary was raised), and shirks his moral responsibility by refusing to disclose his experiments to the community around him.

SCIENTIFIC CURIOSITY CANNOT BE SUPPRESSED

In response to Carlin's call for a "Luddite Humanism," one must ask several questions. Do we really know what "hu-man nature" is? Is it necessarily "dehumanizing" to attempt to eliminate certain genetic defects? Might not curiosity and a desire to alter the genetic code for the betterment of hu-mans be itself a central aspect of "human nature"? Today, with the increased work being done in such areas as brain research, the human genome project, and artificial intelli-gence, these questions are especially pertinent. It is fool-hardy to call for a Luddite Humanism—we can't go back. What inspires researchers to attempt the cloning of human embryos is a combination of curiosity and compassion, the Promethean virtues. Mary Shelley's novel is more relevant than ever, and we need to take its lessons to heart, and call for an increased public discussion of these issues. Joseph Fletcher, the humanist laureate who developed the field of situation ethics, was far ahead of his time in doing this. See his book *Humanhood: Essays in Biomedical Ethics* (Prome-theus, 1979) for thoughtful essays on the ethics of genetic en-gineering, recombining RNA, brain research, and other con-temporary topics.

Regarding the question of hubris, then, I can think of no better response than that of the late science writer Lewis Thomas, who wrote:

Is there some thing fundamentally unnatural, or intrinsically wrong, or hazardous for the species, in the ambition that drives us all to reach a comprehensive understanding of nature, including ourselves? I cannot believe it. It would seem to me a more natural thing, and more of an offense against nature, for us to come on the scene endowed as we are with curiosity, and naturally talented as we are for the asking of clear questions, and then for us to do nothing about it, or worse, to try to suppress the questions. This is the greater danger for our species, to try to pretend that we are another kind of animal . . . and that the human mind can rise above its ignorance by simply asserting there are things it has no need to know. This, to my way of thinking, is the real hubris, and it carries danger for us all.

It is "Luddite Humanism" that is the real danger in a time of technological advancement like we have never experienced before. We cannot wish away the "Frankenstein Impulse"—we must instead try to channel it in a democratic and ethical direction.

Frankenstein's Self-Centeredness Leads Inevitably to Self-Destruction

Arthur Paul Patterson

In yet another of the many modern interpretations of *Frankenstein* as a twist on the ancient Greek myth of Prometheus (the god who defiantly gave fire to humans), scholar and writer Arthur Paul Patterson suggests that Victor Frankenstein exhibits a "Promethean" personality. Patterson loosely defines "Prometheanism" as a tendency to be impatient with limitations and to defy conventional traditions and authority to get one's way. Prometheans, he says, who dominate most affairs in Western society, tend to be self-centered and incapable either of taking full responsibility for their actions or of understanding or expressing love between equals. Patterson's essay is therefore a warning, as, he says, Mary Shelley's book was and remains; but the warning is less against the dangers of tampering with the secrets of life than against allowing one's inner drives and desires to dominate one's life and the lives of others.

I don't think that it is inconsequential that my heroes are men.... It is not because women are not as passionate, creative, or in any way undeserving that they don't make my short list of heroes. Rather, it is because I share with most men an inclination toward "Prometheanism". I don't know why it is not as prevalent in most women. Perhaps it is the hard-wiring of centuries of birthing and caring for life (if I am allowed that stereotypical explanation). I do not think it is because women are morally superior to men, only that they are not as inclined toward Prometheus. I should condi-

Excerpted from "The Passions of Prometheus," by Arthur Paul Patterson, published at www.watershed.winnipeg.mb.ca/mopassions.html (1998). Reprinted by permission of the author.

tion that by saying "at least not yet"; the more women take on patriarchal [male-oriented] perspectives, the more they tend to contract patriarchal viruses.

Men, and animus-directed [masculine-acting] women, have a tendency to follow the "thief of fire" Prometheus. By that I mean that we, like the titan of old, are impatient with any limitations, we feel that the universe is withholding from us something we deserve, and that the only way to get fire is to steal it. Once we are intoxicated by the quest, we will stop at nothing, even the prospect of our own destruction, to get what we want. Above all, we see our pursuit of forbidden fire as wholly virtuous and innoculated from criticism. The Promethean fever causes us to be dangerously out of touch with reality through the misuse of imagination and creativity. Mary Shelley was prophetically astute in portraying a male scientist as her modern Prometheus. Male scientists have nearly destroyed our world through their theoretical imagination rooted in the penetration of the mystery of nature, all the while posturing as benefactors of humanity.

WALTON'S ARCTIC QUEST

Robert Walton, the proto-Prometheus in Mary Shelley's novel, loved the sea. From the time he sat in his Uncle Tom's library reading tales of discovery, through the exhilaration of his first boat trip with a few friends on a native river, to his successful first stint on a Greenway whaling vessel, Walton dreamt of becoming a famous explorer. He would benefit humankind through bringing the mysteries of the Arctic to the light of scientific reason. It was his hope that, in the land of the midnight sun, he would discover the source of magnetism and the Northwest Passage. He was convinced that these treasures would be his reward for persistence and willing suffering.

As his ambition grew, his goal became an Arctic grail quest; his scientific voyage became a spiritual pilgrimage by which he sought to transform the mundane into the miraculous. Robert Walton, the sea-captain transmuted into Sir Walton, the discoverer's version of a Knight Templar fighting for human dominance against the elements.

Margaret Saville, Robert's cultured and married sister, was a surrogate parent and moral guide to him along with Uncle Thomas. Her name means Pearl or Jewel (Margaret) —and town (Saville). This, along with the fact that her initials are M.S., like Mary Shelley's, strikes me as Mary's endorsement of her perspective, which in her 1818 preface she [actually Percy Shelley] defines as an exhibition of amiableness of domestic affection, and the excellence of universal virtue. Margaret Saville represents civility, community and kindness coupled with deep love and concern. This is not to say that Margaret is indulgent; the letters begin with a struggle between her and Robert over the wisdom of the voyage. Margaret takes her dead father's place in attempting to dissuade Robert from becoming an explorer. Combining domestic kindness with the authority of the father, she draws out much nervous and defensive chatter from Walton. He is anything but community oriented or respectful of his father's wishes. Walton, as his name suggests, is a "walled-town", or resistant to differences.

Robert's Promethean qualities are revealed letter by letter. At first his main intention is to assure his sister that he is in control, he is concerned with the safety of his ship and the crew, and that he is thoroughly prepared and deserving of a successful voyage. To assure his sister of the relative safety of the voyage he presents the farthest Arctic as a sailor's Shangri-La [paradise], a temperate zone near the polar ice cap.

> I try in vain to be persuaded that the pole is the seat of frost and desolation; it ever presents itself to my imagination as the region of beauty and delight. There, Margaret, the sun is for ever visible its broad disc just skirting the horizon, and diffusing a perpetual splendor. There—for with your leave, my sister, I will put some trust in preceding navigators—there snow and frost are banished; and, sailing over a calm sea, we may be wafted to a land surpassing in wonders and in beauty every region hitherto discovered on the habitable globe.

He prefers masculine fantasy to the practical, cautious voice of his sister.

There are cracks in his self confidence, as he readily admits. He believes himself to have no friend and that there are no candidates for a relationship with him among his surly crew. He notes that there is one man, his first mate, with character, kindness, and sacrificial values but that he is, nevertheless, an untutored boor of little refinement. The first mate is too different from Walton to establish relationship. Walton says,

> What a noble fellow! you will exclaim. He is so; but then he is wholly uneducated; he is as silent as a Turk, and a kind of ignorant carelessness attends him, which, while it renders

his conduct more astonishing, detracts from the interest and sympathy which otherwise he would command.

WALTON DISCOVERS VICTOR FRANKENSTEIN

Fate has it that Robert does meet someone who provides the sort of friendship he desires, someone who attracts his sympathy, who is scientifically educated, eloquent, sophisticated, and who is, by no means, silent. Victor Frankenstein and Robert Walton cross Arctic paths. Robert all but falls in love with Victor. He admits that he would like to "possess" him as his friend. Such will never be the case, since friendship would require relationship to another, something which Victor and Robert, as dedicated Prometheans, have never learned. Nonetheless, Walton is overwhelmed with Victor's refinement, with his noble suffering, verbal eloquence and total dedication to his task. In effect, Walton has discovered his idealized self in Victor Frankenstein.

In the last few letters, Frankenstein mentors Robert in the ways of Prometheus. He seems at first to be warning him of the dangerous consequences of unbridled passions; but, in the end, does so with such ambivalence that the Promethean way becomes even more attractive to Walton. Victor's final words to his comrade breathe ambiguity,

> Seek happiness in tranquility, and avoid ambition, even if it be the only apparent innocent one of distinguishing yourself in science and discoveries. Yet why do I say this? I have myself been blasted in these hopes, yet another may succeed.

Not only does Victor encourage Walton to follow his own urge to stretch the limits of his crew, and himself, but he refuses, even in death, to release his own project. Victor subjects his newly acquired acquaintance to more danger, and elicits a vow from Robert that he will kill the creature. Frankenstein intended that Walton would continue his mission of destruction, even after his death. He is asking Walton to collude in an immortality project that isn't even his own. Walton is now in the position of his crew, who also have been asked to give their lives for the obsession of Captain Walton. The crew, as collective as they are, have the wisdom to refuse. Upon the threat of mutiny, reluctantly, and with learning very little about what is at work in his soul, Robert returns home to his sister.

What is at work in the souls of men that makes Prometheans of most of us? Isn't that the question Walton is asking when he describes his own self ignorance?

> There is something at work in my soul which I do not understand. I am practically industrious—painstaking;—a workman who executes with perseverance and labour:—but besides this, there is a love for the marvelous, a belief in the marvelous, intertwined in all my projects, which hurries me out of the common pathways of men, even to the wild sea and unvisited regions I am about to explore.

Because he is more like us, less of a titan than Victor, Robert is a good example of how men can get ensnared in Prometheanism. He still has some desire to communicate to his sister, some relationship with the feminine, and is far more aware of his flaws than the intoxicated scientist from Geneva. Looking at Walton, with a side glance at Victor, I detect the following connections between Robert and modern men.

MISUSE OF IMAGINATION

Walton's "can do" machismo is rooted in his fantasy of limitlessness. "I can do anything I put my mind to," seems to say it well. Mary Shelley's dad, William Godwin, said it eloquently, "There is nothing that the human mind can conceive that it can not execute." Prometheans think that by sheer will power they can conquer our own ignorance and pride and perform tasks that are beyond their competence. There is nothing more threatening to them than impotence. Since they fear castration and weakness, they imagine ourselves heroes.

On the mundane level, if men can't put up a drape, fix something mechanically wrong with our car or computer, then we assume there is something deeply wrong with us or perverse in the world. The Prometheus in us tells us that we can drywall, run a marathon, fix plumbing, or write an "out of this world" book, find the Northwest Passage or create a human life. . . .

FOCUSED ON THE IDEAL NOT THE REAL

Prometheans express bravado about what they can do as long as they keep focused on the ideal and are dissociated from the material world. Walton's reliance on the Arctic Shangri-La mythology, which was proposed by the Royal Navy at the time, is an example of refusing to look at the evidence. Imagine the shock as he found himself walled in by ice that threatened to crush his ship. Frankenstein is enamoured by the theoretical. In his mind, he was creating long-lived beautiful creatures who would be eternally grateful for their parentage. Talk about an idealistic parent.

Prometheans can talk about the way to do things and what might be the best solution to a complex problem with confidence, as long as they don't have to apply their knowledge. Once their ideals fall into reality, the birdhouse they were going to build looks like a Homer Simpson Special, a funny, ill-constructed, mockery of their intentions. The grand novel resembles a primary school essay that doesn't hang together very well, and is filled with banality—"and then . . . and then . . . and then. . . ."

IMPLICATE OTHERS IN THEIR SCHEMES

Walton is not safety conscious. He risked the lives of his crew. In one of his later letters to Margaret he has to admit, "Yet it is terrible to reflect that the lives of all these men are endangered because of me. If we are lost, my mad schemes are the cause." However late, Robert's realization is superior to that of Victor who completely exonerates himself. "During these last days I have been occupied in examining my past conduct; nor do I find it blamable." If I consider myself a great mechanic and fix your car's brakes without knowing exactly how to do it, without checking with those who do, I put your life at risk because of my inflated ego. If I fiddle with the intricacies of the operating system of your computer without accuracy and understanding, I place your hard drive in jeopardy. If I set myself up as a spiritual director or counsellor and try to guide you by the seat of my pants through self conceit, I have done irreparable spiritual harm to you and myself. Even in the not so significant decisions, when motivated by an overstretched self opinion of greatness, we harm others around us, through our imagination. We let people down, disgrace ourselves, and ruin the environment. Walton and Frankenstein disregarded the safety of their friends and family to innocently pursue their ideals. Everyone suffered. . . .

LIMITED SELF-REALIZATION

As much as Walton mourns what has happened to Frankenstein, he is still willing to repeat the pattern that resulted in so much death and destruction. He is willing to turn back albeit very reluctantly and forced to do so by his mutinous crew. Victor is on the verge of regret when he warns Walton but his consciousness is quickly snatched back when he encourages Robert and his crew to live as he did. It wasn't the wrongness of the task, the inability to accept human limitation. No, Frankenstein believed, it was a lack of willfulness in himself. He says maybe someone else will be able to achieve what he couldn't. The shame from past Promethean endeavours propels us into a new cycle of inflation-deflation. Still believing it is just a matter of will or more effort, we pick up and try again. "This time it will work, I know it!" We try again, with the same spirit, the same character but a slightly different set of circumstances. We practice serial monogamy with our projects, forever trying to "steal" fire. We honestly feel we can light up our world by our will and know how.

Watershed for anyone is a place of decision making rooted in consciousness. Doesn't that suggest that it is a place where we have learned from our past? But it is so easy to be tricked into repeating the pattern. Do we have to succeed? Do we have to stand out, be different and exceptional or is it okay to be the limited people we are, standing together and content to learn from our differences and the inadequacies of our lives? Do you love monsters, be they projects that aren't up to our expectations, children and parents who are not perfect, friends with irritating foibles, and leaders who tilt us toward Prometheus? These are the questions that will allow us to check whether we are still infected with the fire-stealing disease.

RELATIONAL NARCISSISM

We have seen how there is no holding back for men with a dream. The novel also reveals how Creature and Creator unbridle each other in the literal sense of killing each other's mates. Nothing can come between them in their relationship, least of all a woman. This could lead to the idea that the "sameness" shared between the Protheans, like Walton—Victor, Victor—Clerval, Monster—Victor is homosexual. They are attracted to other men but not relationally. Protheans merely use others as a means of loving themselves and becoming entirely self sufficient. They do not love another but love themselves through another. Herein lies the root of many men's relational problems. The way that they love is often selfish.

If anyone, especially women, try to reality check our dreams they are considered the Enemy. In reality, they are merely an enemy of our isolationism and inflation. Other men are a threat because we have turned them into competitors. We hate having a so-called friend stand over us and correct our mistakes, making what we find so hard, look easy. On the other hand, we love to play the peacock with the skills we have. We consider the less skilled, less than ourselves. Walton and Frankenstein are both elitist and prefer only the company of Prometheans of the same refinement.

It is difficult to find a friend in the midst of elitism. Only those exactly like us, (or the way we would like to see ourselves) or fondly wanting to be like us, are worthy of our company. We barely see the weakness in ourselves and yet are finely attuned to the inadequacy of others. Imagine being married to, or even to be the sister of, a Promethean male, to be taken in by the dreamscape of idealistic fantasies. To be considered a possession or reflection of them. In short to be used. To watch as their high-minded projects end in ruin. To be beguiled by sympathy of such a noble creature who is doomed to a cycle of inflation and deflation. And yet, to love so selfish a creature. Would a Margaret, or a Mary be able to contain a man's desire for stolen fire?

Mary Shelley didn't provide healing for her modern Prometheus, even though she alluded to a perspective which would ameliorate [correct for] the effects of "fire intoxication." Her subtle message is that an appreciation of the moral guidance of the feminine, is a significant part of the answer. The qualities of earth relatedness versus heavenly preoccupations, the acceptance of death and limitations versus immortality through a project, and the ability to look past outward appearances are necessary for sympathy and community. Most of all, the solution is rooted in the willingness to love each other in the context of community or family. She warned us that this was the purpose of her book, back in the preface, exhibition of amiableness of domestic affection, and the excellence of universal virtue.

EROTIC LOVE IS SELFISH

If love is the cure, what kind of love is it? Surely, Prometheans have love and passion—apparently to destructive excess. What Prometheans need is to allow themselves to be loved and guided by a complementary Other. I didn't say "Mother" I said "Other". That would imply that there is a sense of separation and equality in the relationship. Fusion will not cure; in fact, it is part of the problem. . . .

There are two basic kinds of love that we bring into marriage and relationships: Eros and Agape. Erotic love is the passion for possession of another or abandonment of the self to another. In Erotic love inequality is assumed; one or the other partner collapses into the psyche of the other. . . .

If you are contained by another, you are expressing the abandoning aspects of Erotic love. If you desire control over another you are expressing the possessing aspect of Erotic love. It is interesting that Erotic love is usually expressed in dialectic way, where one time you are wanting to possess; and another time, you are wanting to be possessed. The first stance leads to a wilfulness and violent aggression whereas the second expression of Erotic love tends toward passivity and weakness. Erotic love in both its extremes is an expression of Prometheanism.

IMAGINE THE POSSIBILITIES

Remember, however, that this sort of love can be applied to either our tasks or another person in our life but in the end is purely self centered. This is the love Mary saw modelled by Percy Shelley. It is the kind of love where very virile men declare how they possess their women and their projects when things are going well, and yet, when abandoned they become whimpering children in need of a mother.

Mary Shelley advocated another model of love . . . "agapic" . . . the love between two equal but complementary partners, dedicated to working out their psychological growth through an appreciation of difference. This is the model that she hoped for, never experienced, and eventually, saw as not possible as long as we are Promethean in attitude. Her final statement on a lifetime battle with Prometheus is [her 1826 novel] *The Last Man* which reveals that she is pessimistic about the possibility of Agape challenging Eros as a form of love that will sustain our families and the human family at large.

Imagine the possibilities, if agapic love dominated in *Frankenstein: or The Modern Prometheus,* or in our relationships for that matter. What if the Creator and the Creature had a separate existence of mutual respect, if we treated our children as equals who were Other than us, if women and men supported, corrected, and most of all, respected one another? Would our projects really lose their quality or become better? Would we become domestic drones or valued parts of a community? All we need to give up is our wilfulness and our weaknesses, our obsession with self sufficiency, and the belief that we have been cheated by our Creator. Perhaps then we could come to terms with our monsters, with our failures, and our limits. The one word completely missing in *Frankenstein*, and unfortunately also in our lives as well, is the word—forgiveness. Forgiveness is only a reality when there is the acknowledgement of having wronged another. Our task, therefore, is to differentiate from each other, so that we can truly love each other. The nasty part of agapic love is the horrible decree that we must love and take responsibility for our monsters. We must learn to love our children and our projects.

CHAPTER 3

Stage and Film Adaptations of *Frankenstein*

Stage Shows Inspired by *Frankenstein*

Donald F. Glut

Theatrical adaptations of Mary Shelley's most famous work were first produced only five years after the novel's publication in 1818 and have continued unabated to the present. As theater and film historian Donald F. Glut explains in this impressively researched overview of the many stage shows based on the novel, some of these adaptations have taken considerable liberties with the original story and characters.

As early as the first printing of the novel *Frankenstein; or, The Modern Prometheus*, the adaptability of the story to the dramatic stage was recognized. At the time it was believed that the book had been written by Percy Bysshe Shelley, since the text contained so many of his atheistic and radical ideas. As Percy Shelley was too controversial to have a novel even suspected of being of his authorship presented on the stage, ideas for dramatizing the story were abandoned.

THE FIRST ACTOR TO PLAY THE MONSTER

By the time of Percy Shelley's death in 1822, Mary Shelley had already become the acknowledged writer of the novel. In 1823 the story was finally adapted to the stage in at least five versions; two serious dramas (with possibly a third yet to be documented) and three comedies.

The first of the 1823 stage versions of the story was the three-act "opera," *Presumption; or, The Fate of Frankenstein* (also known as *Frankenstein; or, The Danger of Presumption* and as *Frankenstein; A Romantic Drama*) written for the theatre by Richard Brinsley Peake. Understandable changes were made in adapting the story to the stage since the novel spanned much of the globe and presented many situations

Excerpted from *The Frankenstein Legend: A Tribute to Mary Shelley and Boris Karloff*, by Donald F. Glut. Copyright © 1973 by Donald F. Glut. Reprinted by permission of the Scarecrow Press.

impossible to set or perform on a stage. (The changes were indicative of future interpretations of the novel that would appear in other media.) Peake's changes might have seemed drastic, especially to people living in 1823 familiar with the novel. Elizabeth was no longer Frankenstein's fiancée; she was his sister. Frankenstein's love interest was Agatha de Lacey. The scientist was given a superstitious servant named Fritz who, unfortunately, was allotted too much time on stage performing his bits of comedy. James Wallack played Frankenstein.

Thomas Potter Cooke, the reknowned stage villain whose portrayals included devils, sinister monks, killers, and even Lord Ruthven, the bloodthirsty anti-hero of Polidori's *The Vampyre*, delighted in becoming the first actor to portray the Frankenstein Monster (or Demon, as the character was called in *Presumption*) . . . which he played 365 times. As happened to Boris Karloff [the most famous modern movie Franken-stein monster] over a century later, Cooke became identified with the role. Cooke's characterization of the Demon was strong, his make-up bizarre. His eyes seemed bright and watery and made a weird contrast against the yellow and green greasepaint that coated his face. The black hair was very long and unkempt. The lips were black and usually held in a rigid position. The arms and legs were an ugly shade of blue and extended bare from the crude, shroud-like clothing.

Frankenstein had lost his love, Agatha, and because of his grief attempted to create a human being. Fritz had told Cler-val (Elizabeth's intended husband) that his master was en-gaged in a diabolical experiment in the laboratory above the scientist's drawing room. When Frankenstein was about to bring the creature to life as a storm raged from without the house, Fritz spied on him through a window.

FRANK - (*within*) It lives! It lives!

FRITZ - (*jumps down*) There's a hob - a hob-goblin - and 20 feet high - wrapped in a mantle. Mercy - mercy.

falls down. Frankenstein rushes in.

FRANK - It lives. It lives. I saw the dull yellow eye of the crea-ture open - it breathes hard - and a convulsive motion agitates its limbs.

he looks with terror to the door - fastens it and descends the staircase.

What a wretch have I formed! his legs are in proportion and I had selected his features as beautiful! Oh horror! his cadaverous skin scarcely covers the work of muscles & arteries beneath - his hair lustrous black, and flowing - his teeth of pearly whiteness - but these luxuriances only form more horrible contrast with the deformities of the Demon. . . .

The door of the Laboratory with a crash falls off the hinges, as if forced by the Demon.

FRITZ - oh -oh - (*runs out hastily*)

Music - The Demon appears in the light of the Laboratory - he looks around cautiously, descends the staircase rapidly - surveys the apartment - crosses to Frankenstein, and lays hand upon him.

FRANK - (*starts up*) The Demon corpse to which I have given life!

(*The Demon retreats, but looks at him intently*) Its unearthly ugliness renders it too horrible for human eyes!

(*The Demon approaches him*)

Fiend do not approach me - avaunt or fear the fierce vengeance of my arm wreaked on your miserable head -

Music - Frankenstein rushes to the table and seizes a sword - aims a blow - The Demon catches the sword - snaps it - seizes Frankenstein - throws him violently on the floor - mounts the large window - loud thunder and vivid lightning - The Demon disappears at the window.

THE THEATRE PICKETED

The Demon, as portrayed by Cooke, could not speak but only grunted. Cooke enacted the role sympathetically, as when the Demon displayed his sensitivity to light and air while roaming through the woods. When the Demon attempted to perform acts of kindness for Agatha's blind father, his son Felix and Frankenstein tried to destroy him. The brute looked imploringly at his creator but received in return a bullet from Felix's gun. In desperation, the Demon set fire to the blind man's house, ending the second act.

Unable to express himself verbally, the Demon decided to take revenge upon Frankenstein for not accepting him. First the Demon killed William, Frankenstein's little brother. Then during the wedding of Clerval and Elizabeth, the Monster slew Agatha.

The Demon tried to escape by rowing across the lake and to the mountains. But Frankenstein, no longer concerned with his own life, was in pursuit. The climax of the play was quick.

Demon appears at the base of the mountain. Frankenstein follows.

CLER. - Behold our friend - & his mysterious enemy -

FELIX - See - Frankenstein aims his musket at him - let us follow and approach him.

GYP - Hold masters - If the gun is fired it will bring down a mountain of snow on their heads. Many an avalanche has fallen there.

FELIX - He fires - *Music*

Frankenstein discharges his musket - the avalanche falls and annihilates the Demon & Frankenstein.

The Curtain falls.

The ending only partially satisfied the moralists who had picketed the theatre because of Percy Shelley's atheistic ideas and the concept of man creating man. To remove the pressure, S.J. Arnold, the producer of the play, stated, "The striking moral exhibited in this story, is the fatal consequence of that presumption attempts to penetrate, beyond prescribed depths, into the mystery of nature."

Presumption; or, The Fate of Frankenstein premiered on 28 July 1823 in London complete with its quaint songs that interrupted the dialogue at various points. The play was enthusiastically received. Mary Shelley herself attended a performance of the play and later remarked:

> But lo and behold! I found myself famous. "Frankenstein" had prodigious success as a drama, and was about to be repeated, for the twenty-third night, at the English Opera House. . . . I was much amused and it appeared to excite a breathless eagerness in the audience.

T.P. Cooke, described as "the *beau ideal* of that speechless and enormous excrescence of nature," continued to star in the play, taking it to the English Opera House . . . and to London's New Covent Garden in 1824. Later he presented the drama for the Paris Grand Guignol. In 1825 the play was performed in New York. . . .

The play continued to be revived and finally, in 1830, Cooke tired of the role and gave the mantle of horror to an actor named O. Smith. The latter actor also became typecast as the Frankenstein Monster, so much that the English publication *Punch* referred to him as "Lord Frankenstein" in an 1831 issue.

MAGICIANS AND VOLCANOES

There was another serious theatrical version of Mary Shelley's novel presented the same year that *Presumption* opened. This other 1823 adaptation was simply titled *Frankenstein.* The highly melodramatic play was performed at London's Coburg and Royalty theatres. Finally in 1823 there was a trio of burlesque versions of *Frankenstein.* A tailor named Frankenstein, later referred to as "Frankenstitch" and as the "Needle Prometheus," was the leading character in the first of these, presented at the Surrey theatre. This Frankenstein created an artificial man from the corpses of nine workmen. He skillfully applied his talents with needle and thread, salvaging the best parts of the nine bodies. The second comedy was *Frank-in-Steam,* in which an ambitious student stole a body and thought he had brought it back to life. What the student did not know, however, was that his "corpse" had never actually died but had been buried in a cataleptic state. The play was enacted at the Adelphi theatre. The third of these comic plays, presented at the David-Royal Amphitheatre, had a Parisian sculptor give life to a statue of [the ancient Greek storyteller] Aesop, which ran about the stage in the person of a dwarf actor.

A rather offbeat version of Frankenstein was presented in Paris in 1826 at the Gaîté theatre. The play was *Le Monstre et le Magicien* ("The Monster and the Magician") by Merle and Anthony and was again an alteration of Mrs. Shelley's original conception. Instead of showing science to be the means of creating life, it was now the powers of magic. Furthermore the protagonist of the story was changed in name from Frankenstein to Zametti. In *Le Monstre et le Magicien,* the Monster given life by Zametti managed to survive the force of a bolt of lightning, and apparently continued to live through the end of the play, avoiding the traditional spectacular death. The play was translated into English that same year and was performed at the West-London Theatre. In the role of the Monster was, understandably, the Karloff of his day, T.P. Cooke. . . .

The next opportunity for Cooke to don the guise of Frankenstein's Monster was in the same year he did the English-translated version of *Le Monstre et le Magicien.* The new play, which opened at the Royal Cobourg Theatre in London on 3 July 1826, was *Frankenstein; or, The Man and the Monster.* . . . Written in two acts by H.M. Milner, the drama was based both on Mary Shelley's novel and *Le Monstre et le Magicien.* . . .

Frankenstein; or, The Man and the Monster took even

more liberties with Mary Shelley's story. The play was set in
Sicily, where Frankenstein had left his wife Emmeline and
their child, and where he had become attached to the household of the Prince del Piombino. The Prince, interested in the
arts and in science, found favor with Frankenstein's genius.
Frankenstein's laboratory was located in a pavilion given to
him by the Prince. It was here that Frankenstein recited
monologues as heavy-handed as those in the original Mary
Shelley novel:

> SCENE SECOND. (*2nd Grooves.*) *A nearer view of the outside of
> the Pavilion, appropriated as Frankenstein's study - practicable
> door, and transparent window above (dark).*
>
> Enter FRANKENSTEIN *from the Pavilion.*
>
> FRANK. It comes—comes! 'tis nigh—the moment that shall
> crown my patient labours, that shall gild my toilsome studies
> with the brightest joy that e'er was yet attained by mortal man.
> What monarch's power, what general's valour, or what hero's
> fame, will rank with that of Frankenstein? What can their
> choicest efforts accomplish, but to destroy? 'Tis mine, mine
> only, to create, to breathe the breath of life into a mass of pu-
> trifying mortality; 'tis mine to call into existence a form con-
> ceived in my own motions of perfection! . . .

The novel *Frankenstein* was certainly a spectacle with its
grand locations. The play, *Frankenstein; or, the Man and the
Monster* provided its own, though different, spectacle in the
final scenes. The Monster had fled with his two human victims into the mountains. Pursuing the Monster was a posse
made up of peasants and led by [Frankenstein's servant]
Strutt. The Monster had tied Emmeline, using a rope taken
from his waist, to a pillar of rock. He began to lumber toward
her child as Frankenstein ascended the wall of the mountain. Frankenstein pleaded with the Monster to spare his
child, but the living horror indicated the wound given by
mortals. Then Emmeline's ingenuity provided the solution
to Frankenstein's plight as she managed to take a small fla-
geolet [flute] from under her dress and began to play. The
music soothed the savage beast. The Monster went through
a series of deep emotions until he was forced to lie down
from exhaustion. . . .

The final scene of the play brought creator and created together for a last encounter. The Monster was climbing up
the side of the crater of Mount Etna, an active volcano seemingly on the verge of eruption. (The impressive prop crater
occupied the middle of the stage.) Fatigued from his wound,

the Monster was unable to put up much of a battle against Frankenstein, who was following him up the rocky incline. As Frankenstein lunged for him, the Monster stabbed him with Strutt's dagger. The lifeless body dropped into the waiting arms of Emmeline. There was no escape now for the Monster, as soldiers and peasantry were swarming about him from all sides. In desperation he climbed toward the apex of the steaming, flashing volcanic crater. As they began to fire their guns, the Monster leapt into the boiling inferno. The curtain fell as Emmeline, Strutt, and the others paid respect to the corpse of Frankenstein.

SOME OFFBEAT VERSIONS

A third play using the Frankenstein theme in 1826 was first presented on October 9 at the Opera Glass. Titled *The Devil Among the Players*, this poetic dramatization featured three characters of horror—Frankenstein (probably the Monster, as Cooke fostered the mistake in calling the creature by its creator's name), Faust, and the Vampire. (Such combining of famous characters into one story became a technique employed in later years by motion picture studios.) . . .

Another comic adaptation was presented on Christmas day in 1849, *Frankenstein; or, The Vampire's Victim*. The play not only featured the Frankenstein Monster, but also Zamiel, another contemporary horror character. The musical called attention to its own divergence from Mary Shelley's book as one actor sang, "You must excuse a trifling deviation, / From Mrs. Shelley's marvelous narration / . . . ." In this drama the Monster was given life in a halo of blue light. Realizing its own wretchedness, the creature roared, "I oughtn't suppress / My raging organ of destructiveness / . . . ." Later the Frankenstein Monster was defeated by the magical power of music. Again music tamed the savage beast, as in *Frankenstein; or, The Man and the Monster*.

One of the most offbeat of all the stage versions of the story was a burlesque by "Richard-Henry" (Richard Butler and H. Chane Newton) titled both *The Model Man* and simply *Frankenstein*, which was presented in 1887 at London's Gaiety Theatre. The young German medical student Frankenstein seemed to have undergone a primitive sex change operation for the character was now played by Miss Nellie (Ellen) Farren. Miss Farren was the Gaiety's top star. Born in 1846, the daughter of Henry Farren and granddaughter of William Farren the elder, both important personages in the history of the theatre, Nellie began her professional career on the London stage when only eight years old and pleased even the most difficult audiences.

In the role of the Monster, "Frankenstein's Invention," was the Gaiety's second greatest star, Fred Leslie. His interpretation of the Monster was hardly terrifying. Leslie combed his hair straight down and wore an outfit including high boots, a large coat with an enormous flower in the lapel, a hat, and a monocle in his eye. His own prominent nose and chin completed the bizarre, comic interpretation. In some scenes the Monster paraded about in the costume of a ballerina. . . .

Apparently vampires were becoming an established part of the Frankenstein mythos as this musical comedy included vampires that plagued the village of Villasuburba in the Pass of Pizzicato. There were other new characters including Spanish bandits, Mary Ann (Emily Cross; later, Maria Jones), also called "A Maid of Mystery," and a goblin (Cyril Maude), a character reportedly so terrifying that he was cut from the script after only a few performances. . . .

In the third and final act of *The Model Man*, the Monster attempted to be admitted into the Junior Vampire's Clubland and kidnapped the heroine. The vampire, and later Frankenstein, tracked the Monster to the Arctic. There the ice weakened the vampire. As Frankenstein and the Monster met, the region was illuminated by "human stars" through the power of yet another fantastic character, Tambourina, Goddess of the Sun (Sylvia Grey). The show ended with the numerous weird characters frolicking about the stage.

FROM STAGE TO SCREEN

In 1927 *Frankenstein* returned to sobriety as Peggy Webling wrote her own theatrical adaptation of the Mary Shelley novel. The play premiered in London that year at the Preston. It re-opened on 10 February 1930 at London's Little Theatre, with Henry Hallat as Henry Frankenstein. Miss Webling had taken the liberty of interchanging the name of Victor Frankenstein with that of his best friend Henry. Hallat played the part with melodramatic gusto, raving how he had created life "no matter by what means."

Hamilton Deane, whose acting debut was with the Henry Irving Vacation Company in 1899 and who had adapted Bram Stoker's *Dracula* to the stage in 1924, appeared in the

1927 *Frankenstein* as the Monster, with discolored flesh and a thick mop of hair. His clothing was covered with a clay-like layer making him resemble the Golem of silent films. (Bela Lugosi also created a Golem-like look for his screen test as the Monster for the 1931 movie, apparently basing his make-up on that of Hamilton Deane.)

The Monster as portrayed by Deane was sympathetic. He was confused by life and death and discovered his humanity through the kindness of a young crippled girl (played by dark-haired Dora Patrick). At the side of a river, the pathetic creature, unaware that death can be caused by drowning, placed the girl's head beneath the water to see her lovely face through the glassy surface. In other scenes the Monster was entranced as he beheld the sun for the first time; he asked why men hated him; and he threw his glass of wine out of a window and then drank water from a rose bowl.

The Monster fell in love with Frankenstein's fiancée. She was captured by him but finally escaped his grasp. When Frankenstein refused to create a female for him, the Monster killed his maker. Then pleading to God for mercy, he waited in the laboratory and allowed a bolt of lightning to end his artificial life. The reviews of this version of *Frankenstein* were only fair. Nevertheless the play was a tremendous success. Hamilton Deane traveled with the show and presented it on alternate nights with *Dracula*, performing the lead roles of literature's two greatest monsters. *The Graphic* for 22 February 1930 said, ". . . it would be idle to pretend that *Frankenstein* is a very noteworthy play. Written with romantic confidence and great volubility, there are times when we wish that the authoress would cut the cackle and come to the monster.". . .

The Peggy Webling dramatization of *Frankenstein* came under the interest of motion picture director Robert Florey, and eventually James Whale, when Universal Pictures decided to film the story. Much of the original script was retained, with a variation of the scene wherein the Monster drowned the crippled girl, and with more changes for the motion picture screen. The script was adapted for the film by John L. Balderston.

Although Peggy Webling died in 1947, her name continued to haunt Universal Pictures—primarily the legal department. The original agreement made between Universal and Balderston and Miss Webling stipulated that they would receive $20,000, plus one per cent of all gross earnings of *Frankenstein*. In 1952 Balderston claimed that their original conception had been used by Universal in all their succeeding Frankenstein movies made over a period of fifteen years. Balderston and the Webling estate wanted to settle the matter out of court. Their lawyers advised them to the contrary. The case was subsequently taken to court. . . .

The plaintiffs asked for due payment for Universal's seven subsequent Frankenstein movies. The studio, however, contended that these films were not based upon the "dramatic composition" (as stated in the contract) of the two writers. A settlement was finally reached in May, 1953. Universal was able to get all rights involving their version of the Frankenstein Monster. In return the studio gave the plaintiffs a considerable sum believed to exceed $100, 000. . . .

ARSENIC AND OLD LACE

A digression from *Frankenstein* in the theatre that bears inclusion here is Joseph Kesselring's "madcap murder farce," *Arsenic and Old Lace* which opened on Broadway in 1941. The three-act play starred Boris Karloff as Jonathan Brewster, a mad, sadistic killer. Although other actors including Bela Lugosi have played that role the part was obviously written especially for Karloff.

Originally Kesselring had intended to write a serious melodrama. But as the play was rehearsed it became obvious that he had created an ingenious farce where an incredible number of murders could be used to get laughs from the audience. The Brewster family was unique in that madness was hereditary. The two sisters, Abby and Martha Brewster, seemed harmless enough. In their compassion for lonely old men, they gave them drinks of elderberry wine (spiked with arsenic), then put the bodies in charge of brother Teddy, who in his belief that he was President Roosevelt buried these "fever victims" in the canals he was digging in the cellar. The most bizarre member of the family was Jonathan Brewster whose face seemed familiar to fans of horror movies with its stitched scars. Jonathan, fleeing from the police because of his murders, returned to the Brewster house with his partner Dr. Herman Einstein.

> ABBY - (*Stepping down to stage floor.*) Have you been in an accident?
>
> JONATHAN - (*His hand goes to side of his face.*) No—(*He clouds*) —my face—Dr. Einstein is responsible for that. He's a plastic surgeon. He changes people's faces.

MARTHA - (*Comes down to* ABBY.) But I've seen that face before. (*To* ABBY.) Abby, remember when we took the little Schultz boy to the movies and I was so frightened? It was that face!
    (JONATHAN *grows tense and looks toward* EINSTEIN. EINSTEIN *addresses* AUNTS.)
EINSTEIN - Easy, Chonny—easy! (*To* AUNTS.) Don't worry, ladies. The last five years I give Chonny three new faces. I give him another one right away. This last face—well, I saw that picture too—just before I operate. And I was intoxicated.

That picture was obviously *Frankenstein.* Mentioning to Jonathan who he resembled could arouse him to murder. "He said I looked like Boris Karloff," Jonathan remarked when asked why he killed one of his victims. When Karloff spoke that line on the stage it was one of the high moments in the play. . . .

Arsenic and Old Lace was extremely popular, running on Broadway alone for 1444 performances. In 1944, Warner Brothers, which had purchased the screen rights to the play, released the motion picture version of *Arsenic and Old Lace,* brilliantly directed by Frank Capra. The film boasted an almost impeccable cast, including Cary Grant as Mortimer and Peter Lorre as Dr. Einstein. An outstanding mistake was the casting of Raymond Massey in the Jonathan Brewster role. Massey wore a make-up emphasizing deep, stitched cuts, sunken cheeks, and straight hair to suggest the Karloff Frankenstein Monster. His performance was perfect in its own right. Yet the role screamed for Karloff himself. Unfortunately, Karloff was unavailable since he was still doing the play on stage and had already demanded too much money for starring in the film.

Karloff was available, however, to star in at least two radio dramatizations of *Arsenic and Old Lace.* The comedy was presented with Karloff on *The U. S. Steel Hour Presents the Theatre Guild on the Air* the same year the play opened on Broadway. On 25 November 1946 Karloff did the play, drastically edited down to a half hour, on *Screen Guild Theatre.* Karloff also did the play twice on television—on *The Best of Broadway* (CBS, 5 January 1955) with Lorre again as Dr. Einstein and on *Hallmark Hall of Fame* (NBC, 5 January 1962) in color. In 1969 the play was updated by Luther Davis as an ABC special. Fred Gwynne (Herman Munster of *The Munsters*) was made-up to resemble a stitched and scarred Karloff and imitated the British actor's voice. The most famous line in the play, however, had been changed to "He said I looked like the Frankenstein Monster." The line seemed pointless, did not produce any laughs and might have been funny had it been "He said I looked like Herman Munster." Karloff had died shortly before this version of *Arsenic and Old Lace* was presented. Without Karloff in the role created for him, the play could never entirely recapture its former charm.

THE LIVING FRANKENSTEIN

The strangest stage adaptation of *Frankenstein* was created by the Living Theatre, a company of the Radical Theatre Repertory, a commune of free-thinking performers directed by Julian Beck and his wife Judith Malina. The Living Theatre originated in the mid-1950s in a Manhattan apartment, the idea of Beck and his wife. At first the company performed "avant garde" plays and Greek classics. While on a European tour, the Living Theatre began to rehearse their spectacle *Frankenstein.*

There was little of Mary Shelley in Julian Beck's version of *Frankenstein.* The play opened with the various cast members seated around "The Victim" (Mary Mary), a girl upon whom they concentrated so that she would be levitated off the stage. If the levitation proved successful there would be no play. If unsuccessful (which was always the case) the play would go on . . . and on, lasting six hours in the uncut version. (An abridged version ran three and one half hours.)

As the girl failed to levitate she was tossed screaming wildly into a coffin. From that point the stage erupted into a series of murders and executions in numerous brutal ways, with the long-haired members of the cast screaming and howling and running through the audience. Dr. Frankenstein (played by Beck) entered the scenes of violence and began to dismember the various corpses so that the dead could be given new life. . . . Blood was pumped into the corpse creation of Frankenstein. A mystical third eye was transplanted to the creature's navel. The first act ended as twenty acrobatic members of the cast draped themselves over a huge scaffold that dominated the stage. Dr. Frankenstein's nurse (Pamela Badyk) shouted, "He's opening his eyes!" Then the actors on the scaffold writhed, the lights dimmed, and the monstrous composite of twenty human beings peered out at the audience with red burning orbs, ending the first of the three acts.

The second act showed Dr. Frankenstein's futile attempt to communicate with the Monster. Instead the Monster slept and the Living Theatre actors portrayed his thoughts. . . .

In the third act the Monster proceeded to kill his way through various members of the cast. . . . At last the creature again encountered Dr. Frankenstein. They attempted to destroy each other but resulted in exchanging kisses. . . .

Except for the creation of the Monster from parts of corpses, the Living Theatre's *Frankenstein* took little from Mary Shelley. What the play continuously emphasized was that our society was conceived in violence and thrived upon it to survive. Only by reconstructing society through peaceful revolution can man escape his violent nature. The creature of Frankenstein was not destroyed at the end of the production. As we have all contributed to the creation of the Monster, it is also our task to contend with it—or destroy it. . . .

FRANKENSTEIN PUPPETS AND ICE SKATERS

The Frankenstein Monster has continued to be featured on the stage, even as a character in puppet shows like *Les Poupées de Paris.* During the 1940s a stage actor acquired the rights to use the name Karloff, doing a comedy act as "Tony Karloff, the Son of Frankenstein." When the monster stars of *Abbott and Costello Meet Frankenstein* did a personal appearance stage tour in 1948 actor Glenn Strange wore the first in the line of Don Post rubber Frankenstein masks. Other shows at the time advertised their Monster as portrayed by Strange, who along with Universal knew nothing of the deception. Strange learned of the fraud when members of his family wanted to see him backstage and were flatly refused entry.

The Monster was featured in countless live horror shows that played motion picture houses in the 1940s, 1950s, and 1960s, oftentimes scheduled at midnight. With names like *House of the Living Dead* and *Terrors of the Unknown* (the latter with North Carolina television personality Philip Morris) and posters boasting "Alive! ! ! On Stage! In Person! Direct from Hollywood! FRANKENSTEIN MONSTER!" the various monsters appeared after a performance of stage tricks by Magicians called Dr. Evil (Morris), Dr. Satan, Dr. Silkini, and others. The monsters appeared at the end of the show and were always disappointing. The Frankenstein Monster was never more than someone in old clothes and a Post mask.

Sometimes a film strip of lightning (usually the familiar shot from *Bride of Frankenstein*) was projected on the screen. The lights dimmed to total darkness and eerie music sounded through the public address system as the monsters stalked toward the audience. It is questionable whether or not they ever entered that audience made up of screaming girls and boyfriends who proved their courage by throwing whatever was in their hands. One such show that played Chicago claimed that its Frankenstein Monster was played by the stuntman who doubled Karloff and Lugosi in that role. The claim was never verified nor disproven.

When the Twentieth Century-Fox horror film *The Fly* was first released in 1958, actors "flown in from Hollywood" were made up as various famous creatures including a green-faced Frankenstein Monster. The monsters rushed down the theatre aisles to avoid the usual barrage of flying popcorn boxes and rubberband-propelled paper clips. In the 1950s the Strip City burlesque house in Hollywood did a musical show titled *Frankenstein and His Bride*. In a Halloween show Larry M. Byrd played the Frankenstein Monster and did his own Karloffian make-up. The dormant Monster was carried on stage in a coffin. Suddenly the Monster came to life, broke his bonds, strangled the announcer, and lumbered toward the audience. A skating Frankenstein Monster was featured in the 1970 *Ice Capades*. And the Monster was spoofed in a comedy scene presented in 1972 at the Birdcage Theatre of Knott's Berry Farm, Buena Park, California.

The story of Frankenstein and his Monster was first dramatized on the stage. In that medium the legend became popular entertainment. But most of those early versions would be virtually forgotten by the time Mary Shelley's classic was adapted to the motion picture screen.

Transferring the Novel's Gothic Sensibilities to the Screen

Wheeler Winston Dixon

Mary Shelley's compelling and often horrific tale of a man who creates a living creature in his own likeness was a natural, and, as subsequent developments have shown, seemingly endless source of material for filmmakers. University of Nebraska scholar Wheeler Winston Dixon here chronicles the major entries in the extensive Frankenstein filmography, beginning with the famous "lost" 1910 silent version, and including the series, or cycles, of "Frankenstein" films made by the Universal and Hammer Studios, as well as some ambitious, more recent versions that are more faithful to Mary Shelley's original vision. The only important entry missing from Dixon's essay, written in 1990, is British actor-director Kenneth Branagh's 1994 version (with Branagh as Frankenstein and Robert De Niro as the Monster).

While not every college student has had the opportunity to read Mary Wollstonecraft Shelley's *Frankenstein*, most students have seen one or more of the many filmic versions of her novel. Since some students bring to their first reading of *Frankenstein* considerable experience with these cinematic adaptations, instructors should understand the history of the films, including the technological and the economic factors that strongly influenced the form in which they were produced and released. Although this brief essay does not touch on every film version of *Frankenstein*—to say nothing of the many other genre films that partake of the themes explored in the novel (often without acknowledging it)—it does discuss the four major periods to date in *Frankenstein*'s filmic career.

THE "LOST" 1910 VERSION

The first film adaptation of *Frankenstein*, released on St. Valentine's Day, 14 February 1910, by the Thomas A. Edison Company, was directed by J. Searle Dawley, with Charles Ogle as the monster. For more than sixty years, the film was thought to be lost. It was generally assumed that the film's negative had failed to survive the twin dangers of cellulose nitrate decomposition and haphazard archival storage. Then, after more than half a century, the film surfaced in a private cinema archive. After all the years of neglect, it was found to be in surprisingly good condition, with little negative damage. Even before this discovery, some publicity materials were available on the 1910 *Frankenstein*, including a few production stills—one a closeup of the monster . . . and the production "pressbook." From these documents . . . historians were able to get a fairly good idea of what the production looked like. The pressbook features a scene-by-scene description of the film, with the complete text of all the intertitles used throughout the work. The film runs 975 35mm feet or about eleven minutes at today's standardized projection speed of twenty-four frames a second and tells the story of the novel in twenty-five individual tableaux [set-ups, or scenes], each of which advances the plot with dizzying speed.

The rediscovered 1910 Edison film is still not generally available for private or public viewing; indeed, even in 1987, most film histories were still treating the film as lost. However, two sequences from the film, both in their original color tints, were incorporated in the 1976 British television series *The Amazing Years of Cinema* (episode: "The Monsters"): the scene of Frankenstein writing a letter to Elizabeth on the eve of his creation of the monster and the creation sequence itself. My comments here are based on the pressbook materials and a viewing of excerpts from the 1910 film.

In the first shot of the film, an interior scene of a room, Frankenstein leaves his home for study at the university. In the very next shot, we have jumped two years into the future, and Frankenstein, working in the college laboratory, "has discovered the mystery of life" (the quote is from the pressbook). In the film's third shot, Frankenstein is shown writing his betrothed: "In a few hours I shall create into life the most perfect human being that the world has yet known." We see a close-up of the letter in Frankenstein's hand, followed by a wide shot of Frankenstein in his study, rising from his chair, confidently striding off to create his "most perfect human." However, the film tells us, "Instead of a perfect human being, the evil of Frankenstein's mind creates a monster." In shots 5–18, the bulk of the film, we see Frankenstein synthesizing a monster in a gigantic, smoldering vat, as the film alternates shots of Frankenstein's reactions with shots of the "monster forming," in color tints of orange and yellow painted directly on the film (color photographic film had not been invented yet). Frankenstein's laboratory is a . . . chamber of horrors. A human skeleton is tossed on a chair to the left of the frame; the set is dominated by an enormous cauldron at the back, framed on either side by riveted metal doors. This is no temple of scientific experiment: it is an alchemist's lair, echoing Mary Shelley's mention of [the medieval alchemists] Cornelius Agrippa, Albertus Magnus, and Paracelsus in the novel. Frankenstein hurriedly mixes some fluids and powders in an earthen bowl, consults a manual for a moment, and then pours this mixture into the vat. The mixture explodes in a flash of smoke and flame. He spoons more material into the cauldron, exultantly closes the doors, and waits for the Creature to materialize. As he peers through the peephole, we suddenly see from Frankenstein's point-of-view the monster's creation. . . . The use of reverse-motion footage allows the skeletal form of the monster to assemble out of nothingness. As the smoldering, infernal Creature is born, Frankenstein is unable to control his sense of triumph. Watching the monster being created from the slime and mire of a gigantic, steaming tub, we see flesh compose on bone, eyes find sockets, limbs take on human aspect: the sequence proceeds like a magic ritual. The supernatural overtones are more apparent here than in any later version of the novel. . . . This is a graphic, harrowing, and convincing sequence. Many exhibitors found the film too horrid to show their patrons: it is easy to see why.

In shot 19, the monster shambles through a doorway to confront his creator, and we are told by the intertitle that "Frankenstein [was] appalled at the sight of his evil creation." The creation sequence abruptly ends, and in the next shot we see the sleeping Frankenstein tormented by nightmares of the being he has created. In shot 21 Frankenstein returns to his home; the monster has apparently followed him because in shot 22 the intertitles tell us that "haunting his creator and jealous of his sweetheart, for the first time the monster sees himself." The description of the accompanying action tells us that "Frankenstein sees monster. Monster sees himself in glass and struggles with Frankenstein tearing from his waistcoat the flower that his fiancée had given him." This brief evidence of infantile jealousy is the only real conflict we see between Frankenstein and his creation. The next shot, number 23, jumps forward to the night of Frankenstein's wedding, with the intertitles announcing that "on the bridal night Frankenstein's better nature assert[ed] itself." We see "Frankenstein [being] congratulated by his friends," followed by the film's final two shots, as described in the pressbook:

> [T]he monster broken down by his unsuccessful attempts to be with his creator enters the room, stands before a large mirror holding out his arms entreatingly, but gradually the real monster fades away, leaving only the image in the mirror. A moment later Frankenstein enters.

> Standing directly before the mirror we see the remarkable sight of the monster's image reflected instead of Frankenstein's own. Gradually, however, under the effect of love and his better nature, the monster's image fades and Frankenstein sees himself in his young manhood in the mirror. His bride joins him, and the film ends with their embrace, Frankenstein's mind now being clear of the awful horror and weight it has been laboring under for so long.

This brief film presents little more than a sketch of the novel. The Edison Company noted in their pressbook that they had "carefully tried to eliminate all the actually repulsive situations, and to concentrate upon the mystic and psychological problems that are to be found in this weird tale.". . .

THE FAMOUS 1931 KARLOFF VERSION

In 1931, James Whale directed the first sound version of *Frankenstein* for Universal Pictures, under the supervision of the producer Carl Laemmle, Jr. The script of the 1931 film had a rather convoluted genesis. The original novel was in the public domain and so could be used by anyone. Universal, however, based its version of *Frankenstein* on an Americanized version of Peggy Webling's 1930 London stage play of the novel and then brought in John L. Balderston (who had worked with Hamilton Deane in adapting his play of *Dracula* for Universal earlier in 1931) to help with the screenplay. . . . Mary Wollstonecraft

Shelley does receive a credit, although it is not one that I suspect she would be overly fond of: "From the novel of Mrs. Percy B. Shelley." The finished film script has little in common with her novel, but it is still an effective, if slightly dated, piece of gothic filmmaking, highlighted by Boris Karloff's adroit performance as the monster and by the atmospheric, forced-perspective sets used throughout the film. With this 1931 film Whale created a series of iconic [formulaic] conventions that rapidly became clichés in the decade and a half that followed and that, until the advent of the 1957 and 1976 productions, severely limited any serious approach to the novel's actual concerns.

That said, one must acknowledge the many successes of the film. Whale executes beautiful dolly or tracking-camera shots, unusual for the early sound period, that allow the camera to float among the actors, participating in the action it records. Karloff effectively evokes sympathy and empathy for the monster, who is not allowed a single line of dialogue and who could easily have been rendered an insensitive brute. The sets, strongly influenced by the 1919 German film *The Cabinet of Dr. Caligari*, present a nightmarish . . . backdrop for both indoor and outdoor sequences. Although there are a few genuine outdoor scenes, most of the film was shot indoors to allow Whale precise control of the lighting and sound recording. Whale also has an excellent sense of dramatic pacing, which, for the first half of the film at least, keeps the plot moving forward with grisly assurance. In the first reel, Henry Frankenstein (Victor in the novel) is a near-demonic presence, maniacally dedicated to proving his theory that he can give life to an artificially constructed human being. The first ten minutes of the film reveal that Henry is willing—even eager—to exhume freshly buried corpses, to cut down executed criminals from the gallows, or to break into a medical school auditorium to steal a human brain, all in order to create his "child." He is assisted by Fritz, a hunchbacked halfwit ably played by Dwight Frye (who specialized in these roles; he also played the part of Renfield, Dracula's pathetic assistant, in the 1931 film version of Bram Stoker's novel). Henry cuts himself off from fiancée, father, former teachers, and friends to pursue his experiments in a lonely, ruined castle, a visually ideal location for experiments that the film represents as beyond the boundaries of acceptable scientific inquiry. Perhaps the most serious thematic deviation from the novel occurs when Fritz, sent by

Frankenstein to steal a "normal, healthy brain" from the
Goldstadt Medical College, bungles the assignment by drop-
ping the normal brain and makes off with an "abnormal,
criminal brain" described as exhibiting a "distinct degener-
ation of the frontal lobes." Because the brain comes from the
skull of a brute who led a life of "violence, brutality, and
murder," the unfortunate creature who receives it should be
doomed to a similar existence. But Karloff's monster acts
quite reasonably throughout the film, killing Fritz only after
being continually tormented with a lighted torch and sav-
agely whipped by the hunchback. The famous scene in
which Karloff meets little Maria, who shows him the only
kindness in the film, further demonstrates that the plot de-
vice involving the substituted brain is both unnecessary and
inconsistent with the film's own action. Watching Maria
throw flowers in the water, Karloff smiles and laughs for the
first time in the film; when there are no more flowers to be
thrown in the water, the monster reaches out to Maria in a
spirit of childlike play and throws her in the water, thinking
that she, too, will float. Maria drowns, of course, but her
death cannot be construed as an act of violence on the monster's part. It is simply an accident that sets up the final third
of the film, in which the villagers form a lynch mob to
avenge Maria's death. With Henry as one of their leaders, the
villagers track the monster to a windmill, which they set on
fire, ostensibly killing the Creature.

The scene of Maria's accidental drowning was censored
by the Motion Picture Distributors Association of America
(now the Motion Picture Association of America) on the
film's initial release, and this censorship substantially altered both the tone of the film and the director's intent in
staging the scene in the first place. In most surviving prints,
including the one still circulating on home videocassette, we
see Maria and the monster throwing the flowers in the water, then the monster reacting with bewilderment when the
flowers run out, and finally Karloff, with a playful, childlike
smile, reaching in a close-up for Maria. The film cuts at this
point to the villagers dancing in celebration of Henry's impending wedding, and when next we see Maria, she is being
carried as a corpse by her father to the town square, where
he demands that his fellow citizens help him track down the
"fiend" who "murdered" her. The footage of the monster
playfully tossing Maria into the water, her drowning, and the

monster's worried and bewildered response to her misfortune has all been excised. Contemporary industry censors "reasoned" that the scene of Maria being thrown in was too horrific to be shown; it would have to be implied. The cut has precisely the opposite effect, making the monster seem a genuinely malicious murderer and not a pathetic and well-meaning creature whose miscalculation has resulted in a child's accidental death. This deleted sequence was exhumed by Universal for their videodisc release of the film in 1987. The reinsertion of these shots alters the film utterly, making the Creature's eventual death an agonizing martyrdom. Indeed, this deleted footage leads one's sympathies to rest entirely with the monster and not with Henry, who is seen at the film's end recovering in bed while his wife Elizabeth caresses him, secure in the lap of bourgeois luxury. The restored, complete, and uncensored version is now readily available in videocassette and 16mm formats: one hopes that Universal will now add this newly discovered footage to all the available versions.

UNIVERSAL'S MANY SEQUELS

The Bride of Frankenstein, produced in 1935, immediately succeeded the 1931 production. James Whale again directed, but the film is discernably a baroque exercise, shamelessly camped up rather than sincerely felt. Even at this relatively early stage in filmmaking, sequels had become calculated, cynical enterprises, dictated predominantly by the first film's resounding success at the box office. By far the most interesting thing about *Bride* is Elsa Lanchester's double role. In the opening sequence she portrays Mary Shelley, pressed by both Lord Byron (Gavin Gordon) and Percy Shelley (Douglas Walton) to relate "what happened next" after the monster's supposed demise in the 1931 film. Lanchester's appearance at the end of the film as the bride of the monster is one of her most indelible pieces of work as an actress: she remained identified with it for the rest of her long career. But Karloff's performance as the monster and the film as a whole are both badly undermined by unnecessary and tedious additions and digressions. . . . Significantly, compared with the original film, this film did very little business at the box office. Moreover, Karloff, after only one more sequel, abandoned the character of the monster permanently. . . .

Before continuing on to the 1957 British production *The Curse of Frankenstein*, I need to say a few words about the balance of the Universal Frankenstein series. In rapid succession, Universal produced *Son of Frankenstein* (1939); *The Ghost of Frankenstein* (1942); *Frankenstein Meets the Wolf Man* (1943); *House of Frankenstein* (1944); *House of Dracula* (1945), in which the Frankenstein monster appears in a brief cameo; and finally and ignominiously [shamefully], *Abbott and Costello Meet Frankenstein* (1948). *Son of Frankenstein*, directed by Rowland V. Lee, featured Karloff for the last time in the role of the monster. Despite its good cast, including Basil Rathbone, Lionel Atwill, and Bela Lugosi, the film is even more formulaic than *The Bride of Frankenstein*. Apart from a few good scenes—those involving the monster's kidnapping of Frankenstein's child and featuring the dependable Lionel Atwill as the local police inspector whose arm has been "torn out by the roots" during the monster's previous rampages—the film is flat and obligatory. By the time of the film's release Mary Shelley's monster was associated more with the Universal mythos than with the Greek legend whose Prometheus features in the novel's subtitle. The studio became increasingly dependent on trotting out the Frankenstein monster, as well as Dracula and the Invisible Man, at regular intervals to generate much-needed cash.

By the time *The Ghost of Frankenstein* appeared in 1942, Universal had become a different studio altogether. . . . By the 1940s, the Universal Studio had become completely identified with the production of B horror films, some good and some bad, and with the long-running Abbott and Costello series. *The Ghost of Frankenstein* was . . . hopelessly hampered by a short shooting schedule and its low budget. *Frankenstein Meets the Wolf Man* (1943) demonstrated that Universal no longer had confidence in just one monster to bring in people at the box office. The film . . . is simply an atmospheric rendering of by now very familiar territory. *House of Frankenstein* (1944) and *House of Dracula* (1945) . . . gather the Frankenstein monster, Dracula, the Wolf Man, and other assorted Universal properties into ridiculous assemblages of slightly more than an hour's length apiece. Whatever dignity the series once possessed was completely sacrificed in these last two films and particularly, in 1948, in *Abbott and Costello Meet Frankenstein*. In this last film, Dr.

Frankenstein does not even appear: the monster has by now entirely subsumed the identity of its creator. In the film, Dracula supervises the monster's ritual return to consciousness. Clearly, the series had long ago abandoned any hope of coherence or continuity. . . .

THE FIRST HAMMER VERSION

In 1957, Hammer Films, a British production company with studios at Bray, England, produced the stylish *The Curse of Frankenstein*, starring Peter Cushing as Baron Victor Frankenstein and Christopher Lee as the monster. Directed by the gifted British gothicist Terence Fisher, from a script by James Sangster, this was the first color Frankenstein feature and the first that did not use [famous makeup artist] Jack Pierce's patented Universal design for the monster. Much has been written about the Hammer production company. . . . Simply put, Hammer revived and rejuvenated the classic horror films of the 1930s and 1940s, taking them far more seriously than Universal did its original films except for Whale's first *Frankenstein* (1931). Apparently audiences in 1957 were ready for a new wave of gothic horror films quite unrelated to the Universal cycle. Then, too, since many viewers were unfamiliar with the older Frankenstein films, Hammer found an opportunity to reinvent the iconic structure of the earlier series. Like Universal, Hammer followed *The Curse of Frankenstein* with numerous sequels. For most viewers, however, this first film in Hammer's Frankenstein series is the most successful. Although *The Curse of Frankenstein* does not follow the plot of the novel with great fidelity, it nevertheless seems more in tune with the world of Mary Shelley's work than any of the films (save, perhaps, the 1931 original) in the Universal series do.

The Curse of Frankenstein did incorporate two of the basic tenets of the Universal 1931 screenplay: the defective brain—this time a brain damaged during a laboratory fight but used nevertheless—and the unspoken but still clearly delineated concept of the nobility of the Frankenstein family. Peter Cushing, magnificent as Frankenstein, is even more aristocratic than Colin Clive had been. A former member of the Royal Shakespeare Company, Cushing had apprenticed with [the great British stage and film actor] Laurence Olivier and had spent many years on the London stage before venturing into television and films fulltime in the mid 1950s. Christopher Lee, who was to have a considerable effect as Dracula in Terence Fisher's *Horror of Dracula* in 1958, had been working in films since the late 1940s. . . . At six feet, two inches tall, Lee had found it difficult to get leading parts, but for the Creature's role his gaunt, towering figure proved ideal. Lee's makeup, by Philip Leakey, was designed to be as repellent as possible, with acid-scarred skin, stitches running randomly over the Creature's face, and flaps of excess flesh dangling from hands and neck.

Director Fisher and his cast and crew lavished immense care on the production of *The Curse of Frankenstein,* using sets and costumes that were as accurate to the period as possible. The laboratory sequences . . . have a convincing early nineteenth-century air about them. Leyden jars and chemical storage batteries abound in the laboratory set, and the electricity used to revive the monster combines lightning and artificial electricity generated by a primitive spinning-wheel generator. Although the flavor of the film's physical details is scrupulously maintained, this is primarily an actor's film. Peter Cushing's performance as Baron Victor Frankenstein dominates the proceedings. The film's central interest resides in Frankenstein's continuing attempts to re-animate the dead and in his willingness to sanction moral and ethical liberties in doing so. Unlike Colin Clive, who seemed in the grip of a mad, feverish desire that invariably crumbled during the climax of each of the James Whale films, Cushing is unremittingly arrogant, foppish, superior, and chillingly self-centered in the Hammer series. In his creation of the monster, Cushing's Frankenstein is assisted not by a half-witted hunchback but rather by talented members of the medical profession whom he coerces into submission. The Baron's unwilling assistant, Krempe, in *The Curse of Frankenstein* is simply the first in a long line of medical students, country doctors, and retired professionals whom Cushing manages to bend to his will. Moreover, Cushing's Frankenstein does not hesitate to murder his mistress . . . when he tires of her, by the simple expedient of locking her in a room with the monster, who obligingly dispatches her. . . . To obtain a brain for his creation, Frankenstein arranges the "accidental" death of one of his more illustrious colleagues, Professor Bernstein. His murder of Bernstein is so coldly calculated that any audience sympathy for Frankenstein's character evaporates from that point forward: with this act, he has sealed his generic fate. In his final moments in the prison cell, Cushing's Frankenstein begs Krempe to corroborate his story of the monster's creation and subsequent rampage, yet Krempe refuses further complicity, knowing that his refusal will ensure Frankenstein's execution, which is richly deserved. In many of Terence Fisher's films, friendship—and the sacrifices and responsibilities it entails—emerges as a dominant theme. Because Frankenstein callously breaches the limits of friendship and loyalty, he earns the deadly retribution that Fisher's film delivers to him.

Christopher Lee's interpretation of the monster (called "The Creature" in the film's opening titles) is entirely different from Karloff's. In the first film, Karloff was allowed a few grunts or growls when he was menaced with Fritz's torch or a childlike whimper of pleasure when he made friends with Little Maria. Lee's monster is a shambling, mute agent of destruction, whose first act on being brought to life is the attempted murder of Frankenstein by strangulation. Frustrated in this attempt, he escapes to the countryside, where he immediately and without provocation murders an old blind man and his young son. Lee's monster is simply that—a monster—and the audience never builds up any sympathy for, or identification with, his characterization. In view of Cushing's pervasive hold on the narrative, Lee's portrayal does not emerge as a serious defect in the film's construction. If the monster had been given the power of speech, however, he could well have emerged as a formidable counterbalance to the machinations [schemes] of Frankenstein. Fisher does explore this possibility in the later Frankenstein films, but these efforts suffer from the sense of mechanical repetition that pervades most sequels, and the creation-versus-creator conflict is never fully or convincingly developed.

MORE FAITHFUL ADAPTATIONS

In 1973, as the Hammer cycle was winding down with the production of Terence Fisher's *Frankenstein and the Monster from Hell* (the last film of the Hammer Frankenstein series and Fisher's last film as director), a 200-minute adaptation of *Frankenstein* was made for television, entitled *Frankenstein: The True Story*. Although the telefilm was well acted by James Mason, David McCallum, Michael Sarrazin, John Gielgud, and Leonard Whiting, it was overlong, and Jack

126   *Readings on* Frankenstein

Smight's direction did little to help matters. Whiting did his best as Frankenstein, while Sarrazin was intermittently effective as the monster. *Frankenstein: The True Story* suffers from the same defects as most television miniseries: it is poorly paced, slowly plotted, and designed primarily to get the most out of the "name" cast through the use of interminable sequences of static exposition. . . .

In 1976, a small Swedish company, Aspekt Film, produced *Victor Frankenstein* (titled *Terror of Frankenstein* in the United States), a theatrical feature film that was considerably better. Although it suffered from poor distribution in its initial United States release, the film has since been shown extensively on television, attracting some well-deserved, serious critical attention. *Victor Frankenstein* is, quite simply, the best screen adaptation to date of Mary Shelley's work. Aspekt Film and director Calvin Floyd managed to make the most of a very small budget by taking Hammer's physical production strategy one step further: the film was shot entirely on location, without any new sets at all. Costumes, dressings, and technical props are reduced to a minimum. Per Oscarsson's makeup as the Creature is understated, and the film eschews shock effects and standard horror-film iconography almost entirely. More important, the production follows Shelley's novel *more* faithfully than any other film version. At the beginning, Frankenstein is picked up by Robert Walton, the captain of an explorer vessel temporarily icebound on the way to the North Pole. After a brief convalescence on board, Frankenstein relates his story to the captain in flashback. The balance of the film follows Mary Shelley's scenario almost without variation.

Per Oscarsson's monster speaks, from the moment of its creation: the Creature in *Victor Frankenstein* behaves with all the moral complexity with which Mary Shelley originally endowed it. Desperately lonely, jealous of Frankenstein's family and associates, the Creature Oscarsson portrays is a cunning, instinctively evil child—determined to get what it wants, no matter the cost. Karloff and Lee had done yeomanly service with an essentially mute role; in *Victor Frankenstein*, Shelley's monster is allowed to speak, act, and reason as a separate entity, with free will and mobility. For the first time, it emerges as an intellectual adversary, not just a physical brute whose intelligence is ruled by infantile rages and fears. This is a truly horrific creation. . . . Dressed in rough garb, with stiches running around his wrists and neck, thick black lips, and yellow, watery eyes (just as Mary Shelley specified), this solitary, isolated humanoid is fiercely jealous both of his creator and of Frankenstein's link to the rest of humankind. He is the ultimate outsider, unique and terrifyingly alone. . . .

With Floyd's film, the Frankenstein series moves away from the excessively stylized approach of the earlier versions, toward a naturalism that lets the story tell itself without melodramatic embellishment. One of the most striking things about *Victor Frankenstein* is its technical and physical simplicity. Stripped of all the traditional filmic trappings that have become associated with the series, the story of Frankenstein is more terrifying: it becomes plausible. In *Victor Frankenstein*, the series finally reaches a level of maturity not approached by any of the other films discussed here. Floyd is content to let the ideas of the novel come through in his work, without resorting to conventional horror-film imagery. He takes his imagistic strategies directly from the novel, not from Hollywood. Paradoxically, for this reason a number of critics have dismissed the film as a faithful, yet uninspired, version of the book. To me the film is inspired, but not by any of its many predecessors. *Victor Frankenstein* places faith in and draws inspiration from the novel itself, succeeding in a way that none of the other versions can: it is Mary Shelley's own vision, faithfully translated to the screen.

Seen Through "Hollywood's Mirror"

Mary Shelley's tale has only been brought to the screen once with even a modicum of fidelity (not counting the 1973 television version). Yet in the 1910, 1931, 1957, and particularly the 1976 productions, the essence of her novel survives the many emendations made to her plot. Even the assembly line of screenwriters who worked on the 1931 production could not entirely abrogate her central themes: the creation of a being from the remnants of human beings; the questions of birth, life, and death and of the immortality of the soul; and the ways in which one's life can be changed irrevocably by research when that research outstrips its human needs. The Edison film, now restored, shows how early narrative filmmakers were fascinated by the novel's central themes: the creation of life and the questions of physical and spiritual life and death. The Universal and Hammer films, imperfect though they are, do address many of the central issues of Mary Shelley's work, and thus they can serve as an incomplete, yet tantalizing, introduction to the novel. *Victor Frankenstein* demonstrates how a faithful production of the novel can in many ways outstrip the previous film adaptations. There will no doubt be many more versions of *Frankenstein.* The summer of 1986 saw a remake of *The Bride of Frankenstein* (entitled simply *The Bride*), with the rock singer Sting as Frankenstein and *Flashdance*'s Jennifer Beals as the bride of the monster. Although the definitive production of *Frankenstein* may be in the future, all the films discussed here may serve as keys to the novel, as seen through the mirror of Hollywood invention or through a faithful adaptation of the original text. The list of these films demonstrates that when the task is approached with taste and skill, it is possible to transfer the gothic sensibility from the novel to the film essentially without compromise—an endeavor I feel certain Mary Wollstonecraft Shelley, visionary that she was, would enthusiastically have approved.

The 1931 Film Makes Frankenstein a Cultural Icon

David J. Skal

Before actor Boris Karloff donned Jack Pierce's now universally recognized makeup for the 1931 Universal film version of Mary Shelley's *Frankenstein,* many plays and films had tried to capitalize on the unique and compelling main concept of the novel. But all of these early adaptations had played to fairly limited audiences. It was the 1931 version, highlighted by Karloff's powerful and often sympathetic portrayal of the Monster, that finally catapulted Mary Shelley's creation into international public consciousness. Ever since, Karloff's makeup and portrayal have remained the quintessential vision of Frankenstein's Monster. And the characters of Frankenstein and his creation, as well as Mary Shelley's concept, have become cultural icons readily recognizable to people of all ages and all educational levels in nearly all nations and cultures. In this way, Mary Shelley's book, which to this day few people have actually read, affects the modern human consciousness to a degree that she could scarcely have anticipated. This informative essay, by literary and film historian David J. Skal, tells the story of how the most famous of all Frankenstein films was made.

One of the most powerful and disturbing images in *All Quiet on the Western Front,* Universal's biggest success of 1930, was a bodiless pair of hands, clinging to a barbed-wire fence, the rest of their owner having just been blown away before the viewer's eyes. Universal produced a similar pair

Excerpted from *The Monster Show: A Cultural History of Horror,* by David J. Skal (New York: Norton, 1993). Copyright © 1993 by David J. Skal. Reprinted by permission of the Malaga Baldi Literary Agency on behalf of the author.

of dismembered hands the following year, and it grafted them onto Boris Karloff for what would become the most famous horror movie of all time.

A one-reel *Frankenstein* had been produced by Thomas Edison in 1910; another, extremely free adaptation called *Life Without Soul* appeared in 1915, and the story was considered by First National [Film Studio] in 1928 as a special-effects vehicle for Willis O'Brien, who had animated the dinosaurs for *The Lost World* and would achieve his greatest fame as the head technician on *King Kong*. The O'Brien conception of *Frankenstein* would have involved a stop-motion monster in miniature, thus allowing for superhuman feats impossible for an actor or stuntman to achieve. The film never got past the planning stages.

ASSEMBLING THE DIRECTOR AND ACTORS

Three years later, Carl Laemmle, Jr., vindicated by the box office success of *Dracula*, proceeded with his plans to film Mary Shelley's *Frankenstein*. Universal had purchased the rights to the John L. Balderston and Peggy Webling [stage] adaptation on April 8, 1931, a scant seven weeks after the release of *Dracula*. Balderston's agent, Harold Freedman, had been unable to extract anything near the $40,000 he had negotiated for *Dracula;* Universal was in terrible financial shape. Artfully, Freedman suggested a compromise: Balderston and Webling would accept a far smaller sum—$20,000, to be precise—in exchange for a one percent interest in *Frankenstein*'s gross earnings as a film. By preempting the stage rights, Universal would be able to produce *Frankenstein* without competition or delay. And having spent good money for the title to a solid and provocative dramatization of a literary classic, the studio then followed time-honored Hollywood procedure: they threw the thing away.

The French director Robert Florey was first announced as the man charged with creating *Frankenstein*, and he developed a script in which the monster emerged as a pure brute, devoid of even the half-articulate pathos [feelings of pity and sympathy] that Balderston and Webling had given it.

Florey was intent on creating a stylized . . . film . . . and filmed a couple of test reels on the standing sets of *Dracula* to show off the style. Bela Lugosi was the reluctant monster, heavily puttied and painted, and possibly with massive wig or headdress. . . . Several accounts of this lost test makeup have been published, and almost all are contradictory. The wig, however, is a persuasive detail in that virtually every description, drawing, or photograph of stage and screen adaptations of *Frankenstein* from 1823 through 1930 present the monster with a flowing, flying, or tangled mane of hair. Lugosi bridled at being assigned a nonspeaking part, and Florey was being eased out of the project by James Whale, a stage director from Britain who had come to Hollywood prominence through three war pictures. . . .

A REVIEW OF THE 1931 FILM

This unsigned review, typical of most of those the film received after it opened on December 4, 1931, appeared in the December 8 issue of the entertainment trade paper Variety.

Looks like a 'Dracula' plus, touching a new peak in horror plays, and handled in production with supreme craftsmanship. Maximum of stimulating shock in there, but the thing is handled with subtle change of pace and shift of tempo that keeps attention absorbed to a high voltage climax, tricked out with spectacle and dramatic crescendo, after holding the smash shiver of a hair trigger for more than an hour.

Finish is a change from the first one tried, when the scientist was also destroyed. The climax with the surviving Frankenstein (Frankenstein is the creator, not the monster itself) relieves the tension somewhat, but that may not be the .effect most to be desired.

The figure of the monster is a triumph of effect. It has a face and head of exactly the right distortions to convey a sense of the diabolical, but not enough to destroy the essential touch of monstrous human evil. Playing is perfectly paced. . . . Boris Karloff enacts the monster and makes a memorable figure of the bizarre figure with its indescribably terrifying face of demoniacal calm, a fascinating acting bit of mesmerism.

Photography is splendid and the lighting the last word in ingenuity, since much of the footage calls for night effect and manipulation of shadows to intensify the ghostly atmosphere. The audience for this type of film is probably the detective story readers and the mystery yarn radio listeners. Sufficient to insure success if these pictures are well made.

Quoted in Donald F. Glut, *The Frankenstein Legend: A Tribute to Mary Shelley and Boris Karloff.* Metuchen, NJ: Scarecrow Press, 1973, pp. 119–120.

After Universal had considered Leslie Howard for the title role, Whale chose Colin Clive, a haunted, highly strung actor who had played the tortured Captain Stanhope in the stage and film versions of *Journey's End*. He realized that Clive's nerve-racked intensity was also the perfect quality for Henry Frankenstein—a man on the edge if there ever was. And Mae Clarke, the prostitute from *Waterloo Bridge*, would be his fiancée, Elizabeth. Finding a monster took a bit longer, however. The new concept of the creature required an actor of some range and sensitivity. Whale's shooting script, by Garrett Fort and Francis Ford Faragoh, used the Florey script as a skeleton, but added a deep note of pathos throughout.

"It does not walk like a Robot," the script took pains to spell out. Its first offscreen sound was to be "haunting, piteous . . . like that of a lost animal."

"I spent ten years in Hollywood without causing the slightest stir," Boris Karloff recalled in later years. "Then one day I was sitting in the commissary at Universal, having lunch, and looking rather well turned out, I thought, when a man sent a note over to my table, asking if I'd like to audition for the part of a monster."

DESIGNING THE MONSTER

Whale's companion David Lewis had suggested that he look at Karloff, who had recently made a striking gangster in *The Criminal Code*. Karloff, the former William Henry Pratt, sometimes drove a truck for a lumberyard between acting assignments. He had no illusions about the film industry owing him a livelihood, and no expectations whatsoever that his name would soon become a household word for horror. Whale thought Karloff's face had interesting possibilities; an amateur painter himself, the director sketched the actor, experimentally exaggerating the bony ridges of Karloff's head. He showed his ideas to Jack P. Pierce, head of Universal's makeup department since 1926. Pierce had been responsible for Conrad Veidt's hideous grin in Universal's *The Man Who Laughs* (1929), based on the Victor Hugo novel, and had created the Lugosi makeup for the Florey screen test of *Frankenstein*.

Pierce was considered a genius by those who worked with him, although perhaps an egotistical one; he never publicly acknowledged Whale's part in developing the

Frankenstein makeup. Perhaps the closest he came to acknowledging the debt was his 1939 comment to the *New York Times*, "I didn't depend on my imagination." He said that he had spent three months of preliminary research in such areas as anatomy, surgery, criminology, and electrodynamics. The final Frankenstein design, he maintained, was a more or less logical result of these efforts.

In retrospect it seems clear that Pierce, and Whale, also drew less consciously on design considerations than from the stylized machine-age aesthetic [visual style] which, by 1931, had . . . elbowed and angled its way into the worlds of advertising, decoration, and industrial design. The movement had begun in 1925 in Paris, at the Exposition Internationale des Arts Décoratifs et Industriels Modernes, and the show's title gave birth to the two names used most often to describe the movement: Art Deco and Art Moderne. American designers further refined the aesthetic, and *Fortune* later recalled that Fifth Avenue shops soon filled their display windows with the "grotesque mannequins, the cubist props, the gaga designs" that would define the style.

"Grotesque mannequin" well describes the Frankenstein monster, an amalgam [mixture] of conventional bodies torn apart and reassembled according to new, logical-angular, electromechanical principles. The square head—a common motif in advertising graphics of the time—powerfully evokes the plight of an old consciousness forced to occupy a new paradigm [mold], a round brain bolted uneasily into a machine-tooled skull. As the script described its structure: "The top of its head has a curious flat ridge like the lid of a box. The hair is fairly short and quite obviously combed over the ridge to hide the defect of the joining where the brain was put in." The monster is a modernist designer's nightmare: the seams show, the clamps and bolts stick out. Form follows function, but just barely.

Beyond Whale and Pierce, various other designers in Universal's production and even in its promotion department had contributed visual concepts for the monster-in-development. Two recurring elements were especially notable: the protruding brow, suggesting evolutionary regression, and the paradoxically futurist design of a completely mechanical man along the lines of "Televox," an automaton developed by Westinghouse Laboratories in the late 1920s. The most "mechanical" concept, by Universal's poster illustrator Karoly Grosz, first introduced the notion of a steel bolt through the neck, a detail that in itself would come to symbolize the total Frankenstein mythos. . . .

The Karloff monster, of course, undermines the principles of the machine aesthetic while drawing inspiration from them; although the creature is decidedly modern, he's certainly not deco—something more, indeed, like a battered hood ornament for a wrecked economy. Like a gargoyle on the Chrysler Building (completed in 1930) the Frankenstein monster is yet another inevitable culmination of the machine aesthetic: a looming and unforgettable piece of vernacular [native] architecture.

"We were all fascinated by the development of Karloff's face and head," recalled actress Mae Clarke, who had a ringside seat at the construction site. "White putty on the face was toned down to a corpse-like gray. Then there was a sudden inspiration to give the face a green tint. It awed us and gave Boris and the rest of us a different feeling about the whole concept." (Karloff himself is said to have suggested the heavily puttied eyelids, which added a dimension of pathos and incomprehension.)

When the makeup was ready for a screen test—in black-and-white—Karloff had no idea how effective the finished product would be. Would it inspire horror . . . or laughter? "I was thinking this, practicing my walk, as I rounded a bend in the corridor and came *face-to-face* with this prop man.

"He was the first man to see the monster—I watched to study his reaction. It was quick to come. He turned white—gurgled—and lunged out of sight down the corridor. Never saw him again. Poor chap, I would have liked to thank him—he was the audience that first made me *feel* like the monster."

CAUGHT BETWEEN HUMANISM AND MECHANISM

The story, as it was filmed, drew freely on a number of sources: the Shelley novel, the films *The Golem* and [*The Cabinet of Dr.*] *Caligari*, and earlier dramatic adaptations of *Frankenstein*. Frankenstein's assistant Fritz (played by Dwight Frye) . . . was first depicted on the London stage in 1823. The character had been revived by Horace Liveright and Louis Cline in their unproduced rewrite of the Balderston script, which they sold to Universal. Liveright's contributions to the modern horror genre, therefore, included not only the resurrection/exploitation of its two major icons, but the popularization of the "laboratory hunchback" motif as well.

Frankenstein's opening credits appear over a half-distinct, demonic face approaching the viewer through a field of wheeling eyes, perhaps inspired by similar designs used on stroboscope discs, the whirling Victorian toys that anticipated the motion picture. The effect immerses the viewer at once in a primal [primitive] kind of experience, simultaneously infantilized and terrified. The opening scene in a cemetery contained what was, for 1931 audiences, a visceral jolt: the sound of earth crashing on the lid of a coffin. The microphone itself was placed in the casket, the better to magnify the reverberations. David Lewis remembered: "The film has been imitated so much that today, these scenes don't bother people. But in 1931, it was awfully strong stuff." At a preview in Santa Monica, some audience members voted with their feet. "As it progressed," Lewis said, "people got up, walked out, came back in, walked out again. It was an alarming thing."

Pieced together from graveyard, gallows, and medical-school scraps, the monster is brought to life in a machine-age orgasm of crackling machinery. In 1818, Mary Shelley had made a passing reference to "a powerful engine"; in 1931, her dream-image took on the pop-sculptural reality of the present. *Frankenstein*'s gleaming lightning-arc generators, created by electrical engineer Kenneth Strickfaden, were a wholly fanciful, high-wattage commentary on the machine age. . . .

Whale's film depicted a monster squarely in the grip of this confusion, a pathetic figure caught, as it were, on the barbed wire between humanism and mechanism. The exact time period is vague—it *seems* to be the present; the women, for instance, wear 1931 fashions, and although the film is "about" science, all of the trappings of technology and industrialization—cars, radio, telephones—are totally absent, as if their energy has been displaced totally into Frankenstein's laboratory equipment. The film is set in a German village, which is also peopled (as if during the war) with characters speaking with British and American accents. Since the village sequences were shot on the same outdoor sets as *All Quiet on the Western Front,* no doubt many audience members experienced a certain level of déjà vu, whether or not they consciously equated *Frankenstein* with the celebrated war picture.

OBJECTIONS FROM THE CENSORS

One of the most famous sequences of *Frankenstein* is one that was not seen in its entirety for almost fifty years. The monster encounters a little girl at the edge of a lake. Unfrightened, she leads him in a game of throwing flowers on the water to see them prettily afloat. The monster, carried away with delight, throws the girl in after the flowers, but unlike the daisies, she sinks and drowns. The scene ended up being radically cut. Karloff insisted in later years that the scene didn't work because James Whale had insisted that he throw the child with a brutal, overhead motion, rather than set her gently on the water. Karloff, who had some back problems, was incapable of hurling the girl very far, and the resulting, compromised action looked buffoonish. Fortunately, just the idea of the child's death was sufficiently upsetting ("No little girl is going to drown in one of my pictures!" Carl Laemmle, Sr., is reported to have fumed to his secretary) so that the scene was cut for many engagements, ending with the monster reaching out for the child (and, ironically, leaving some viewers with the impression that they had been spared the spectacle of some shocking molestation).

Many misconceptions have taken root about the extent of *Frankenstein* censorship in the United States. Most of the notable excisions—the drowning of the little girl, Colin Clive's line "I know what it feels like to be God," etc., were demanded cut by the MPPDA [the movie censors] only upon the film's proposed rerelease in 1937. The six states with censor boards, of course, could, and would, snip as they pleased—Kansas was particularly bad. But in censor-lite California, the film seems to have been shown intact—Clive's "God" line, for instance, was quoted in a San Francisco review. And the drowning scene was apparently still in place when Universal submitted the film to the MPPDA for reissue clearance; the industry censors made their formal objection to it on June 9, 1937. (The scene, found largely intact at the British Film Institute, was finally restored to a videodisc version of *Frankenstein* released by MCA in the 1980s, but still lacks close-ups of the child sinking, etc.—details the English censors marked for excision.). . .

FRANKENSTEIN: JUST WHAT THE DOCTOR ORDERED

Frankenstein, of course, lent itself to novel and outrageous exploitation stunts. In addition to the techniques ushered in by *Dracula*—nurses on duty, free "nerve tonic," and the like—elaborate advance publicity included, in one venue, the firing of a gun backstage to startle the audience out of its collective seat just as the trailer began to play on the screen. Robert Sparks, who managed the Arcadia Theatre in Temple, Texas, advertised for a woman who would agree to sit alone in the darkened theatre for an advance preview of the film in exchange for a cash reward. "Eighty-five women made application for the privilege," reported *Motion Picture Herald,* and the prize finally went to the selfless soul who offered to give her prize to charity. In Omaha, an out-of-control crowd for a midnight screening shattered a theatre's plate-glass window, generating more publicity and interest.

"Morbidity is not without its claim to a high place among humanity's respectable emotional interests," wrote *Motion Picture Herald* in its discussion of *Frankenstein.* The film had arrived, "if the psychologists can be believed, at the familiar psychological moment. Say the savants, people like the tragic best at those times when their own spirits are depressed, and the economists tell us that even more than their spirits are at a low ebb."

Frankenstein, evidently, was just what the doctor ordered.

Hammer's Frankenstein Cycle Emphasizes Both Old and New Themes

Peter Hutchings

The celebrated British motion picture studio Hammer Films produced its now world famous Frankenstein horror cycle between 1957 and 1973. By the time Hammer decided to tackle *Frankenstein*, says Peter Hutchings of the Department of Historical and Critical Studies at the University of Northumbria at Newcastle, a considerable "Frankenstein mythos" already existed. Hutchings defines this mythos as the sum of characters, themes, ideas, symbols, and story lines based on the original novel, all of which were and are circulating in the public domain and consciousness. Striving to add something new and different, Hammer wisely took a unique visual and thematic approach to the Frankenstein mythos, one that in some ways captured the ideas and sensibilities of Mary Shelley's novel and in other ways departed from them. In particular, Hutchings argues, the films in the Hammer cycle tend to revolve around Frankenstein himself, as opposed to those in the earlier Universal cycle, which concentrate on the Monster. Also, the Hammer Frankenstein films heavily emphasize Baron Frankenstein's traits as a patriarchal (father) figure whose arrogance and defiance of societal norms continually bring ruin on himself and those around him. In this respect, Hammer's Baron Frankenstein strongly resembles Mary Shelley's Victor Frankenstein.

In an essay on the various adaptations of *Frankenstein*, [scholar] Paul O'Flinn remarks, 'There is no such thing as

Frankenstein, there are only *Frankensteins,* as the text is ceaselessly rewritten, reproduced, refilmed and redesigned.' If this is true, what needs to be considered is whether relating the various film Frankensteins directly to Mary Shelley's original 1818 novel, or for that matter to a broader eighteenth- and nineteenth-century gothic sensibility, has any explanatory force. . . .

The horror film genre in the form that we understand it today was founded by Universal in the early 1930s. This company established various monsters (Dracula, Frankenstein, the Wolfman, the Mummy) within cycles of films, with their destruction and subsequent reconstitution built into a particular generic pattern that commanded the movement from one film to another. It was this model with which Hammer was working when it commenced its cycles. It invoked a structure, a set of expectations (which involved the names of monsters, aspects of iconography [symbols and styles]) in order that its audience, for whom Universal horror was in many ways the norm, would recognise Hammer's films as belonging to that genre. However, at the same time Hammer worked to differentiate its product from American horror, directing its films at a particular audience. . . .

THE MONSTER'S INDEPENDENT EXISTENCE

Critics dealing with the novel *Frankenstein* and subsequent theatrical and cinematic versions often seem to be searching for elements which link all the works together. For [English film critic] David Pirie, writing about Hammer's early Frankenstein films, continuity is provided through relating these to a gothic tradition which is seen as permeating the last two hundred years of British culture . . . 'Terence Fisher and his collaborators transformed the Baron into a magnificently arrogant aristocratic rebel, in the direct Byronic tradition [i.e., like poet Lord Byron, Mary Shelley's friend], who never relinquishes his explorations for one moment.'

For other critics, there is a continuity in the meanings (psychological and cultural) that run beneath what are in this case seen as historically specific variants of the Frankenstein myth, which itself symbolises and crystallises a modern consciousness of the world.

In an essay on stage and film versions of *Frankenstein,* [scholar] Albert Lavalley attempts to establish what exactly these various adaptations have in common with Shelley's novel: 'they share a vision of man as victim and outcast, innately good and open to the joys of nature and human society, but cut off from positive emotional responses and severed from society, a tormented and pitiful creature.' However, at the same time he also identifies a problem in the adaptive process from book to stage/screen which, regardless of the degree of its faithfulness to the story, ensures that each adaptation of *Frankenstein* can be only partial and incomplete:

> Almost any visualising of the Monster makes him the focal point and a point that is perforce primarily physical. The book may gradually present us with a fully formed human psyche whose feelings, yearnings, and logic are often more profound than those who reject its outward husk, but the stage and film must fix that outward appearance from the very start . . . the problem of make-up in dramatizing *Frankenstein* would remain both an occasion for drama and spectacle and a barrier against the deeper themes of the novel.

What Lavalley recognises . . . is that the visibility of the creature that results from theatrical and cinematic adaptation is necessarily destructive of much, if not all, of the novel's distinctive identity. In particular, what is lost is the way in which in the novel the Monster functions as a sort of tabula rasa, a blank space . . . within and around which various moral and political debates can be staged. In both stage and film versions the Monster or creature is more visibly, materially present, leading its own independent existence, the nature of its monstrosity fixed, there for all to see. . . .

ADAPTING MARY SHELLEY'S NOVEL TO HAMMER'S STYLE

Between 1957 and 1973 Hammer released seven Frankenstein films: *The Curse of Frankenstein* (1957, d. Terence Fisher), *The Revenge of Frankenstein* (1958, d. Fisher), *The Evil of Frankenstein* (1964, d. Freddie Francis), *Frankenstein Created Woman* (1967, d. Fisher), *Frankenstein Must Be Destroyed* (1969, d. Fisher), *The Horror of Frankenstein* (1970, d. Jimmy Sangster) and *Frankenstein and the Monster from Hell* (1973, d. Fisher). Peter Cushing starred as Baron Frankenstein in six of these productions, and his presence was obviously important in binding the films together into a recognisable unity. To this can be added those formal properties which characterised the work of Terence Fisher, who directed five of the seven, and, more generally, what might be termed a studio 'house style'—which included the use of particular settings, actors, etc.—that emerged from the formative activity of the 1950s (and towards which both Cushing and Fisher were extensive contributors).

Hammer's construction of a Frankenstein cycle takes on elements of the pre-existing Universal cycle; most notably, the foregrounding of the name of 'Frankenstein', which is widely recognisable as a generic category, a marketable horror 'star'. In addition, as the cycle develops, a movement or pattern from (re)constitution to destruction becomes evident both within and between films, although in Hammer it is Frankenstein himself, rather than the Monster, who is caught up in and defined through this constitutive-destructive process (but, importantly, not always destroyed at the end of any film). This change of emphasis is connected with and contributes to a wider shift of focus away from concerns of class towards a set of historically determined and specific gender problematics, thereby aligning the Frankenstein cycle with the characteristic concerns of the British horror genre in the 1950s.

The process of product differentiation, of negotiating with a pre-existing version of Frankenstein [specifically the Karloff/Universal version], is most apparent, as one would expect, in the earliest part of the cycle. In fact it is in *The Curse of Frankenstein* and *The Revenge of Frankenstein* that, through this negotiation, a conceptual and thematic framework is established upon which subsequent productions are founded. What these films are doing is articulating the figure of Frankenstein within and making it relevant to a particular socio-historical context, bringing him back to Britain, so to speak.

The opening sequence of *The Curse of Frankenstein*, in which a priest visits the Baron in the prison where he is awaiting execution for a murder (which, we later learn, was actually committed by his Creature) and the Baron proceeds to tell him his story, has a twofold function. First, it invokes memories of the moralistic dimension of the early Universal horror films, the stress laid there on the dangers of straying outside social and moral norms (which, of course, is also an important aspect of the original novel). Second, it explicitly announces a rewriting of the Frankenstein myth, a return to and reworking of origins which will result—as is hinted by the fact that it is Frankenstein himself who tells his own story—in the privileging of the creator over the monster. In this sense, the priest's 'Perhaps you'd better start from the beginning' refers as much to Hammer as it does to the Baron.

This combination of pre-existing and innovatory generic

elements is reiterated [repeated] in the relationship between Frankenstein and his tutor then friend, Paul Krempe. On one level, this reproduces the moralistic element present in Frankenstein's encounter with the priest, with Paul frequently arguing for the social responsibility of the scientist and Frankenstein supporting an idea of 'pure', socially uncommitted scientific research. . . .

In this sense, Victor Frankenstein operates as yet another of Hammer's male authority figures. . . . Clearly he is a very different sort of scientist from the more melodramatically emotional Frankenstein portrayed by Colin Clive in the first two Universal Frankenstein films. . . .

ESTABLISHING AN IDENTITY FOR BARON FRANKENSTEIN

Christopher Lee's Creature, mindless, without speech, malevolent and destructive from its first moment of life (when it attempts to strangle its creator), functions in this respect as a symbol of the antisocial nature of Frankenstein's ambitions. (Of course this is true for Frankenstein films generally, although the forms which this antisocial behaviour takes in Hammer, the deployment of notions of class and gender therein and the way in which all these elements are valued, are specific to Hammer itself.) The dramatic conflict posed here goes beyond any concern displayed in the film about the social responsibility of the scientist, caught up as it is with the more characteristic Hammer preoccupation with male authority. The sort of male authority represented by the Baron—powerful and attractive but also anachronistic [out of date] and disruptive—is shown to be at odds with the more socially viable but far less authoritative and less attractive masculinity embodied in this case by Krempe.

That Frankenstein's experiments involve the displacement of the woman from the processes of biological reproduction suggests . . . the possibility of a non-reproductive female sexuality, although this possibility is ruthlessly circumscribed by a male authority which is dependent upon the woman's silence or submission. So in *The Curse of Frankenstein* Elizabeth is never aware that Krempe and the Baron are struggling over her, never sees the Creature, never even suspects its existence. . . .

The defining opposition between different forms of masculinity is elaborated and refined in *The Revenge of Frankenstein*. In this film, the Baron confronts the medical council.

This, with the exception of Hans who quickly defects to Frankenstein, comprises respected members of the bourgeoisie in a society characterised by immutable class boundaries. That Frankenstein moves freely from his middle-class practice to a working-class hospital, while the council members who at one point visit him in the latter location seem distinctly uncomfortable in the presence of the proletariat [workers], underlines the Baron's separateness from social structures. At the same time these same council members are shown as being weak as regards their domestic authority over their wives who continue to visit the fashionable Baron Frankenstein despite the council's disapproval of him. (A similar moment occurs in *The Curse of Frankenstein*, where the burgomeister, a symbol of male social authority, is given us as a hen-pecked husband when he appears at the Baron's eve-of-wedding reception.) . . .

As with *The Curse of Frankenstein*, the heroine Margaret is a troubling element in the relationship between Frankenstein and his male assistant. Like Elizabeth in the earlier film, Margaret tempts the assistant away (although only temporarily in this case) as well as intruding into spaces where she is not made welcome by the Baron (the laboratory in the first film, the hospital in this). However, the Creature is substantially different, human and articulate, serving a different end, for here, in a fully realised urban and non-feudal setting (which can be contrasted with the feudal castle that provides the main location for *Curse*) the humanness of the 'creature', the way in which, initially at least, it . . . looks no different from human beings, functions both as an expression of the Baron's need to disguise himself and his research . . . and as an eloquent commentary on the Baron's own inhumanity, the impossible demands he makes upon the human body. In line with this, Hammer's 'monsters' are often more human than their creator. The scene in which Carl, his body deteriorating, bursts into a party and screams out Frankenstein's name, thereby revealing his identity to the members of the bourgeoisie present, perhaps shows most clearly the key element in Hammer's version of Frankenstein, the necessary and inevitable exclusion of the Baron from the essentially bourgeois social order that he, through his nature and his experiments, disrupts and threatens. . . .

By the end of the 1950s, Hammer had succeeded in establishing an identity for the Baron. This was in part signalled through Peter Cushing's authoritative performance, but, crucially, it also involved the construction of a set of class and gender relations, within which the actions of Frankenstein were positioned, defined and valued. The Baron's aristocratic title served to place him in relation to the invariably bourgeois society within which he was compelled to live and work. . . .

THE CULMINATION OF THE HAMMER CYCLE

The Hammer Frankenstein formula as sketched out here, with the Baron defined in relation to the monster, the woman and other men, does seem to offer more opportunities for development than does the Universal Frankenstein cycle. In the latter, the Monster, 'a shambling goon with a forehead like a brick wall and a bolt through his neck', its appearance and status fixed from the start, stumbles from one film to another. In Hammer's cycle, however, there are substantial changes of emphasis from film to film, with these changes signalled through the different ways in which each film identifies the creature (more often than not human) and the woman (increasingly foregrounded). This in turn permits an increasingly eloquent interrogation of all the values that the Baron represents, one which ensures the cycle's continuing vitality and social relevance. . . .

Terence Fisher's . . . *Frankenstein Created Woman* (1967) and *Frankenstein Must Be Destroyed* (1969) together mark one of the creative highpoints of the British horror genre, systematic and uncompromising explorations of the potentialities and limitations of Hammer's conceptualisation of Frankenstein.

Frankenstein Created Woman opens with an ominous low-angle shot of a guillotine. The execution which follows—throughout which the liveliness of the condemned is favourably contrasted with the meaningless words of an accompanying priest and the brusqueness of the guards—suggests that the social order which provides the film's setting is a particularly repressive one. In line with this, in the later trial scene, in which Hans, Frankenstein's young assistant, is accused of a murder of which he is innocent, those in positions of social authority, most notably the police chief, are shown as vindictive, petty, self-important and ignorant. . . .

Perhaps not surprisingly when located within such a context, Frankenstein becomes a more sympathetic figure than he is at any other point in the cycle; indeed many of the police chief's undesirable qualities are made apparent through

Frankenstein's resistance to them in his appearance before the court. However, these sympathetic qualities need to be seen as arising from a weakening of that absolute and arrogant male authority which previously in the cycle had characterised Frankenstein's actions. That such a shift has taken place is made clear by the nature of the Baron's first appearance in the film. He emerges deep-frozen from a coffin-like box, a willing object of one of his own experiments ... with the gloved hands that cover his face signifying an uncharacteristic degree of passivity and subjection. Consequently the Baron is far less threatening to a social order than he is elsewhere. He seems more concerned to create a space for himself where he can work undisturbed, showing little interest in money. . . .

So while a familiar opposition between aristocratic decisiveness and bourgeois pettiness and ineffectuality is reiterated here, much of the pre-existing mutual animosity has been siphoned away. A key factor behind this change, which is also an engagement with a possibility already present within Hammer's Frankenstein cycle, is the transformation of the woman from passive object to problem subject. Her being moved centre-stage causes other elements in the film to be revised, so that what previously had been a contest between different forms of masculinity becomes an investigation of the basis upon which masculinity in general is founded—namely sexual difference, itself understood in terms of a particular masculine positioning of the woman. . . .

Like *Frankenstein Created Woman, Frankenstein Must Be Destroyed* opens with a decapitation, although in the first film this is a socially sanctioned act, against which the Baron to a certain extent stands opposed, while in the second it is Frankenstein himself, in search of fresh body parts, who is responsible. The change of attitude towards the Baron thereby registered—also apparent from the film's title, which transforms him from what was previously a creative subject to an object requiring destruction—is underlined by Frankenstein's first appearance after the decapitation when, wearing a disguise, he grapples violently with a burglar who has strayed into his laboratory. Here Frankenstein himself, through the grotesque mask that is his disguise, is seen as monstrous. Moreover, the physicality of the fight, with glass smashing and, at the end, a human head being kicked across the floor, signals a move away from the poetic abstraction of *Frankenstein Created Woman* to a more characteristic (for

Hammer) physically orientated realism. . . .

As has already been noted, Hammer's Frankenstein is defined in relation to particular understandings of society, the monster and the woman; and it is through shifts in this network of relations (alongside subtle modifications in Cushing's performance and appearance—an increased iciness and darker hair, the latter signifying here a renewed vitality) that the Baron is repositioned and revalued. . . .

A consideration of the position of the woman in *Frankenstein Must Be Destroyed* shows that the film has a twin focus. On the one hand, it is the story of Frankenstein's endeavours in the field of brain transplantation, his authoritative search after knowledge. But on the other hand, it is also about Frankenstein's subjection of the film's heroine Anna (with the romance between Anna and Karl providing the link between these two aspects); and it is in the relation between these two strands, which are only tenuously connected within the narrative itself, that the film establishes its position regarding the particular type of authority represented by the Baron. At this point one can in fact argue that while the earlier *Frankenstein Created Woman* presented a tentative exploration of the possibilities—and eventual impossibility—of female subjectivity within the cycle's constitutive structures, *Frankenstein Must Be Destroyed* stands as a reaction against this, a self-destructive implosion by which the certainty and sense of professional purpose which had characterised earlier Hammer productions . . . is restored, but only at the cost of the explicit destruction of the woman, an act which enables the hero/professional to come into being and at the same time marks him as completely, irredeemably monstrous. . . .

In a sense, the Frankenstein cycle as a whole can be read as a paradigm for much wider changes in the genre that were made as a response and contribution to a historical transformation of gender identities. . . . *Frankenstein Created Woman* and *Frankenstein Must Be Destroyed* . . . function as a bridge between British horror of the 1950s and the 1970s version, which would prove to be more open ended, less dependent upon an absolute male authority. Frankenstein's destruction at the end of *Frankenstein Must Be Destroyed* can be read in this way as a symbolic and necessary casting out, opening the way for a potential distancing from a patriarchal authority conceived by this stage as utterly monstrous.

CHRONOLOGY

1797

Mary Godwin (later Mary Shelley), daughter of the controversial writers William Godwin and Mary Wollstonecraft, is born in London on August 30; the mother dies ten days later.

1798

Britain's Admiral Nelson defeats the French navy in the Near East.

1801

William Godwin marries his neighbor, Mary Jane Clairmont, whose children by a previous marriage—Charles and Jane (later called Claire)—bring the number of children in the Godwin household to four (counting young Mary's half-sister, Fanny Imlay Godwin).

1804

Napoleon proclaims himself emperor of France.

1812

War erupts between Britain and the United States; Mary leaves home for an extended stay at the home of a family friend, William Baxter, near Dundee, Scotland.

1814

Mary returns to London; she comes to know poet Percy Bysshe Shelley, who has recently become a regular visitor to the Godwin home; she and Percy (accompanied by Claire) run off together to the Continent in July; they return to London in September.

1815

Napoleon is defeated at Waterloo and goes into exile; Mary gives birth to a daughter, who dies, unnamed, a few days later.

1816

Mary's and Percy's son William is born; Mary, Percy, William, and Claire travel to Geneva, Switzerland, in May and rent a house next door to Lord Byron, the renowned poet; Mary begins writing *Frankenstein* in June; in October, Fanny Imlay Godwin commits suicide; two months later, Percy's wife Harriet is found drowned; three weeks after Harriet's death, Mary and Percy are married in London.

1817

American writer Henry David Thoreau is born; Percy Shelley loses custody of his children by Harriet; Mary finishes writing *Frankenstein* in May; in September, she gives birth to a daughter, Clara.

1818

Mary publishes *Frankenstein* anonymously in March; young Clara dies in September.

1819

The American vessel *Savannah* becomes the first steamship to cross the Atlantic Ocean; Spain cedes Florida and the Oregon Territory to the United States; in June, young William Shelley dies (of malaria or possibly cholera); Mary gives birth to another son, Percy Florence (who will become her only child to survive to adulthood), in November.

1822

The elder Percy Shelley accidentally drowns in a boating accident off the western Italian coast.

1823

The second edition of *Frankenstein* is published; the first stage adaptation of the novel, titled *Presumption; or, The Fate of Frankenstein,* is produced; Mary collects and edits Percy's unpublished poems; she also publishes her novel, *Valperga or the Life and Adventures of Castruccio, Prince of Lucca,* and her short story, "A Tale of Passions."

1824

John Quincy Adams is elected president of the United States; Byron dies in Greece; Mary publishes Percy's poems as *Posthumous Poems of Percy Bysshe Shelley.*

1825

Mary receives and refuses a marriage proposal from an American actor.

1826

Mary publishes her novel *The Last Man.*

1831

Mary publishes a revised edition of *Frankenstein,* appending an introduction explaining how she originally conceived the characters and central idea.

1833

The British end slavery throughout their empire; Mary publishes "The Invisible Girl" and other short stories.

1835

Mary publishes her novel *Lodore.*

1836

William Godwin dies.

1837

Princess Victoria ascends the British throne, marking the beginning of a long reign that will come to be called the Victorian age in her honor; Mary Shelley publishes her last novel, *Falkner.*

1840

Mary and her son Percy Florence visit the Continent.

1843

English novelist Charles Dickens publishes *A Christmas Carol.*

1844

English naturalist Charles Darwin publishes *Geological Observations of the Volcanic Islands;* Mary publishes *Rambles in Germany and Italy,* about her recent travels in Europe.

1848

German philosophers Karl Marx and Friedrich Engels write the *Communist Manifesto;* Percy Florence Shelley is married.

1851

Mary Shelley dies in London on February 1; her remains are buried with those of her parents.

FOR FURTHER RESEARCH

MODERN EDITIONS OF THE TWO TEXTS OF *FRANKENSTEIN*

Marilyn Butler, ed., *Frankenstein, or the Modern Prometheus* (1818 text). New York: Oxford University Press, 1994.

Robert E. Dowse and D.J. Palmer, eds., *Frankenstein, or the Modern Prometheus* (1831 text). New York: Dutton, 1963.

Maurice Hindle, ed., *Frankenstein, or the Modern Prometheus* (1831 text). New York: Penguin Books, 1985.

Diane Johnson, ed., *Frankenstein by Mary Shelley* (1831 text). New York: Bantam Books, 1981.

M.K. Joseph, ed., *Frankenstein, or the Modern Prometheus* (1831 text). New York: Oxford University Press, 1969.

Leonard Wolf, ed., *The Annotated Frankenstein* (1818 text). New York: Clarkson S. Potter, 1977.

ANALYSIS AND CRITICISM OF *FRANKENSTEIN*

Stephen C. Behrendt, ed., *Approaches to Teaching Shelley's* Frankenstein. New York: Modern Language Association of America, 1990.

Paul Cantor, *Creature and Creator: Mythmaking and English Romanticism.* New York: Cambridge University Press, 1984.

William Patrick Day, *In the Circles of Fear and Desire: A Study of Gothic Fantasy.* Chicago: University of Chicago Press, 1985.

Judith Halberstam, *Skin Shows: Gothic Horror and the Technology of Monsters.* Durham, NC: Duke University Press, 1995.

David Ketterer, Frankenstein'*s Creation: The Book, the Monster, and Human Reality.* Victoria, Canada: University of Victoria Press, 1979.

Robert Kiley, *The Romantic Novel in England.* Cambridge, MA: Harvard University Press, 1972.

George Levine, *The Realistic Imagination: English Fiction from* Frankenstein *to* Lady Chatterley's Lover. Chicago: University of Chicago Press, 1981.

Christopher Small, *Mary Shelley's* Frankenstein: *Tracing the Myth.* Pittsburgh: University of Pittsburgh Press, 1973.

Mary K.P. Thornburg, *The Monster in the Mirror: Gender and the Sentimental/Gothic Myth in* Frankenstein. Ann Arbor: University of Michigan Research Press, 1987.

Samuel H. Vasbinder, *Scientific Attitudes in Mary Shelley's* Frankenstein. Ann Arbor: University of Michigan Research Press, 1976.

William Veeder, *Mary Shelley and* Frankenstein: *The Fate of Androgyny.* Chicago: University of Chicago Press, 1986.

Susan Wolstenholme, *Gothic (Re)Visions: Writing Women as Readers.* Albany: State University of New York Press, 1993.

STAGE AND FILM VERSIONS OF *FRANKENSTEIN*

Michael Brunas et al., *Universal Horrors: The Studio's Classic Films, 1931–1946.* Jefferson, NC: McFarland and Company, 1990.

Edward Edelson, *Great Monsters of the Movies.* Garden City, NY: Doubleday, 1973.

William K. Everson, *Classics of the Horror Film.* New York: Carol Publishing Group, 1990.

Donald F. Glut, *The Frankenstein Legend: A Tribute to Mary Shelley and Boris Karloff.* Metuchen, NJ: Scarecrow Press, 1973.

———, *The* Frankenstein *Catalogue: Being a Comprehensive Listing . . .* Jefferson, NC: McFarland, 1984.

Leslie Halliwell, *The Dead That Walk: Dracula, Frankenstein, the Mummy, and Other Favorite Movie Monsters.* New York: Continuum, 1986.

Roy Huss and T.J. Ross, eds., *Focus on the Horror Film.* Englewood Cliffs, NJ: Prentice-Hall, 1972.

Peter Hutchings, *Hammer and Beyond: The British Horror Film.* New York: Manchester University Press, 1993.

James F. Iaccino, *Psychological Reflections on Cinematic Terror: Jungian Archetypes in Horror Films.* Westport, CT: Praeger, 1994.

John McCarty, *The Modern Horror Film: 50 Contemporary Classics.* New York: Carol Publishing Group, 1990.

David J. Skal, *The Monster Show: A Cultural History of Horror.* New York: W.W. Norton, 1993.

ABOUT MARY SHELLEY

Betty T. Bennett, ed., *The Letters of Mary Wollstonecraft Shelley.* 3 vols. Baltimore: Johns Hopkins University Press, 1980–1988.

Kenneth N. Cameron, ed., *Romantic Rebels: Essays on Shelley and His Circle.* Cambridge, MA: Harvard University Press, 1973.

Jane Dunn, *Moon in Eclipse: A Life of Mary Shelley.* London: Weidenfeld and Nicolson, 1978.

Paula Feldman and Diana Scott-Kilvert, eds., *The Journals of Mary Shelley, 1814–1844.* 2 vols. Oxford: Clarendon Press, 1987.

W.H. Lyles, *Mary Shelley: An Annotated Bibliography.* New York: Garland, 1975.

Anne K. Mellor, *Mary Shelley: Her Life, Her Fiction, Her Monsters.* New York: Methuen, 1988.

Elizabeth Nitchie, *Mary Shelley, Author of* Frankenstein. Westport, CT: Greenwood Press, 1970.

Mary Shelley, *Rambles in Germany and Italy, in 1840, 1842, and 1843.* 2 vols. London: Edward Moxon, 1844.

Muriel Spark, *Mary Shelley.* New York: Dutton, 1987.

Emily W. Sunstein, *Mary Shelley: Romance and Reality.* Boston: Little, Brown, 1989.

William A. Walling, *Mary Shelley.* New York: Twayne, 1972.

ABOUT THE SOCIETY AND LITERATURE
OF MARY SHELLEY'S ERA

Marilyn Butler, *Romantics, Rebels, and Reactionaries: English Literature and Its Background, 1760–1830.* New York: Oxford University Press, 1981.

Msao Miyoshi, *The Divided Self: A Perspective on the Literature of the Victorians.* New York: New York University Press, 1969.

Harold Perkin, *The Origins of Modern English Society, 1780–1880.* London: Routledge and Kegan Paul, 1973.

J.L. Talmon, *Romanticism and Revolt: Europe 1815–1848.* New York: Harcourt, Brace and World, 1967.

Philip A.M. Taylor, ed., *The Industrial Revolution in Britain: Triumph or Disaster?* Boston: D.C. Heath, 1958.

Malcolm I. Thomis and Peter Holt, *Threats of Revolution in Britain, 1789–1848.* London: Macmillan, 1977.

G.M. Young, *Portrait of an Age: Victorian England.* London: Oxford University Press, 1973.

INDEX